TRUST
in
The LIGHT

~

I have come as a light to shine in this dark world,
so that all who put their trust in me
will no longer remain in the dark.
John 12:46 (NLT)

~

A study of Jesus through
Matthew, Mark, Luke, John and beyond.

Your word is a lamp for my feet, a light on my path.
Psalm 119:105 (NIV)

Book 1 of 4 in the L.I.G.H.T. series
(L.ife I.n G.od H.olds T.ruth) (John 8:12)

#1 TRUST in The LIGHT (John 12:46)
#2 LIVE in The LIGHT (Psalm 27:1)
#3 REST in The LIGHT (1 John 1:7)
#4 VICTORY in The LIGHT (John 1:5)

JANETTE KIEFFER

Redeeming Grace 99|1 Ministries
1001-A E. Harmony Rd.
#46
Fort Collins, Colorado 80525

TO THE FAITHFUL AND TRUE ONE
(REV. 19:11)

...They lay their crowns before the throne and say: "You are worthy, our Lord and God, to receive glory and honor and power, for you created all things, and by your will they were created and have their being." Revelation 4:10-11 (NIV)

~

...and for Noah Mark, Maryelle Grace, Faith Marie, Micah Matthew, Elijah Christopher, and Joshua David.

You are loved more than words can express.
I have no greater joy than to hear that my children are walking in the truth. 3 John 1:4 (NIV)

I passed on to you what was most important and what had also been passed on to me. Christ died for our sins, just as the Scriptures said. He was buried, and he was raised from the dead on the third day, just as the Scriptures said. 1 Corinthians 15:3-4 (NLT).

CONTENTS

WELCOME

Greetings dear one,

Thank you for meeting me here. I have been praying for you and no doubt have you come to hold this study in your hands but by sheer answered prayer. Prayer that what is written here would honor Him in every way and be an encouragement to His people.

This study will have us dancing to the harmony of the four gospels[i] (Matthew, Mark, Luke and John) and leaping into various other books of the Bible as well because as I'm sure you've heard the Bible is really the very best commentary on itself!

Each of the gospel books "has unique perspectives and theological messages that supplement the others and challenges readers in important ways. God chose to inspire four different writers because each perspective is important for the church."[ii]

As we seek to intimately know our Savior's heart through an in depth study of His Word we will twist and turn the looking glass up into His Light for it is only in His Light that we truly see Light (Psalm 36:9). We will look at the questions and situations others in Scripture posed to Jesus and how each afforded Him another opportunity to reveal more of Who He is and wanted to be to them. In turn might we begin to see our questions, trials, setbacks, failures, triumphs and successes all as opportunities for Him to reveal more of His heart to us!

I'm praying as we climb this mountain of discovery together taking on one "rock" at a time we will at the end be able to look back and see that all those stones have become our stepping stones of remembrance; our Ebenezer's, each one declaring His praise that *"Thus far the LORD has helped us."* (1 Sam. 7:12 NIV). He is faithful!

With a trusting faith emboldened, minds captivated, and hearts enraptured by The King of kings may we never stop climbing our mountain one step at time! To His praise and glory, when we reach the top (and you will) may you find that all those stones have added up to one giant mountain - conquered... because He said, *"Never will I leave you; never will I forsake you."* (Hebrews 13:5 NIV) ... remember beloved, how thus far I have always helped you.

Remember your Ebenezer and keep climbing,
someone needs the Hope you have.

STUDY NOTE on "A Time to Reflect" pages:

At the end of each week a space is created for you to just sit at His feet and abide in His heart as He pieces together all that He speaks to you throughout your week of study with Him. Allow Him to practically apply it to your life in a tangible life changing way as only He could. I am praying He tailor fit His Word to your heart and mind so that the result is beautiful life transformation into more of who He created you to be as a reflection of His Son.

I would also encourage you to consider who God has placed in your sphere of influence that He may have you share what you are learning. The "recipe" you use to share can be aligned to your gifts, abilities and enjoyments… do you like to take walks… use a walk as your "recipe for reflection" with another. Do you like to drink tea or fix cars, bake or plant flowers?! Use what you have where you are at. Do not miss an opportunity to intentionally create a space that you can naturally invite another into.

Follow God's lead as He opens doors for you to share your learnings week to week from His Word. Pray for His wisdom and discernment before even beginning this study that God would go ahead of you to prepare your heart to receive His Word and to fully equip you and provide "recipe of reflection" ideas and opportunities that will honor Him and encourage others - including you!

You shall teach them diligently to your children, and shall talk of them when you sit in your house, and when you walk by the way, and when you lie down, and when you rise. Deuteronomy 6:7 (ESV) Do this so that your children who have not known these instructions will hear them and will learn to fear the LORD your God. Do this as long as you live… (Deuteronomy 31:13 NLT)

Let this be written for a future generation, that a people not yet created may praise the LORD: Psalm 102:18 (NIV)

May grace, peace and living hope be yours in abundance~ Janette

WEEK 1

But these are written that you may believe that Jesus is the Messiah, the Son of God, and that by believing you may have life in his name. John 20:31 (NIV)

Day 1: Remember Who Loves You

Hello! I am not sure how you got here but I am just thrilled, just tickled pink that you have come to this page alongside me! A wise friend shared with me once that nothing happens by chance but rather is just God showing up unannounced! Psalm 52:9 (ESV) comes to mind, *I will thank you forever, because you have done it. I will wait for your name, for it is good, in the presence of the godly.* I am already blessed that He thought to have us meet and I pray that you too are encouraged, and He is honored in every way throughout our time in His Word together.

As we embark on our quest, the aim of our hearts is to truly know our God more in the midst of all our unknowns and to allow the Truth of Who He is to anchor our (all too often) rocking wayward ship to His steadfast and faithful promises. Colossians 1:17 (NIV) *He is before all things, and in him all things hold together.*

Take a moment as we dedicate our time to Him and ask that He lead us and stir up His Spirit within us to a fire ablaze with reverential holy fear. He is unshakable, victorious and almighty! He knows you individually, intricately, intimately, and who knows… that maybe you have come to this study to uncover a depth of His heart... *for such a time as this?"* (Esther 4:14 NIV)

Let us embark, shall we?!

In the beginning the Word already existed. The Word was with God, and the Word was God. He existed in the beginning with God. God created everything through him, and nothing was created except through him. The Word gave life to everything that was created, and his life brought light to everyone. The light shines in the darkness, and the darkness can never extinguish it. (14) So the Word became human and made his home among us. He was full of unfailing love and faithfulness. And we have seen his glory, the glory of the Father's one and only Son. John 1:1-5, 14 (NLT)

The Word is Jesus Christ Himself, the Word made flesh (in the above version it uses the word "human", the Word made human). Jesus is God. He was fully God and fully man while He walked this earth.

Philippians 2:7 (NIV) *rather, he made himself nothing by taking the very nature of a servant, being made in human likeness.*

Please circle the words "made his home" in John 1:14 above. This is the Greek word *skenoo* meaning "pitched his tent". This Greek word is related to the Old Testament *skene* for "tent, tabernacle". Exodus 25:8-9 refers to the place God's glory resided with the Israelites as being in one such a tent or tabernacle. (*NLT Study Bible* notes, pg. 1975) "The Father's glory in the Tabernacle (Exodus 40:34-38) was now present in Jesus Christ (John 2:11, 12:23-28, 41; 17:1-5)."[iii]

Our Creator God's desire from the beginning was to be with us! The sin in the Garden of Eden back in Genesis 3 is what separated us from God. The only way to cross the canyon sin had caused between us was for God to send His Son Jesus to sacrifice Himself in our place; to pay the penalty for our sin otherwise we would be lost forever!

Romans 8:3-4 (NIV) *For what the law was powerless to do because it was weakened by the flesh, God did by sending his own Son in the likeness of sinful flesh to be a sin offering. And so he condemned sin in the flesh, in order that the righteous requirement of the law might be fully met in us, who do not live according to the flesh but according to the Spirit.*

"Fully met in us" and to "live … according to the Spirit" How is that even possible to live free from the power of sin?! Well, let's look at another aligning passage to help shed some more light on the subject.

John 3:16 (NIV) *For God so loved the world that he gave his one and only Son, that whoever believes in him shall not perish but have eternal life.*

Please circle the phrase "so loved the world" in the above verse.
Do you live in this world? _____
Now please circle "whoever believes".
Do you believe in Jesus as your personal Savior and God? _____

Oh, how I am praying that you do. It is never too soon to make the decision to give your life to Jesus dear one. Do not wait until you have it all figured out (none of us is guaranteed the next moment) and who wants a God small enough for our finite minds to figure out completely?! I still don't have it all figured out, that's part of the adventure! Mystery keeps the romance alive does it not?!!

Jesus is the Savior of the world and of my life. He is the one true God and the only Way to heaven. If you do not know Him or have not decided to give your life to Him yet I know He loves you still. But the One who gave His life to give you the free choice to love Him back, to receive the free gift of eternal life in His Kingdom without fear of death because He rose again from the grave victorious -- deserves a decision. It is yours to make, Jesus extends His nail scarred hand to ALL. May you receive Living Hope today and truly LIVE dear one!

Please record the following verses below.
Romans 3:23-24

_____

_____

Romans 5:8

_____

_____

Romans 10:9

_____

_____

John 14:6

_____

_____

To accept Jesus as your God and Savior, simply pray… Dear God, I know I am a sinner in need of a Savior and Jesus, my God, I believe You are it. I believe You died and rose again to save me. I give my life to You. In Jesus name, Amen.

If you made the choice to give your life to Jesus today for the first time, please tell a fellow believer in Jesus to rejoice and share encouragement.

Luke 15:7 (NIV) *I tell you that in the same way there will be more rejoicing in heaven over one sinner who repents than over ninety-nine righteous persons who do not need to repent.*
We asked earlier just before the listing of John 3:16, how is it even possible to live set free from the power of sin.

2 Peter 1:4 (NLT) tells us, *And because of his glory and excellence, he has given us great and precious promises. These are the promises that enable you to share his divine nature and escape the world's corruption caused by human desires.*

What promise do we have on the very inside of us as believers in Jesus, according to 1 Corinthians 6:19-20?

_____

The very power of the Holy Spirit!

Remember our Creator God has ALWAYS wanted a relationship with us… in the Garden of Eden He was there… He was present in the tabernacle out in the wilderness with His people... He tented within human flesh to become the sacrifice, The Way, back to eternity with Him!! NOW having rose from the grave His Holy Spirit tabernacles within us as believers!!!! He has imputed His divine, sin overcoming nature within us as believers in Jesus!

The cost of that free gift is only free because of a love so great that it surpassed our lack of ability to repay. We could and can do nothing to earn this gift. On the cross Jesus said, *"It is finished!"* (John 19:30 NIV) He gave up His life and rose again to give us an eternal life fully paid for - just believe and receive dear one, never forget Who loves you - always and forever.

As we work our way through this study the next few weeks together, we will be digging through the gospels or the books of the Bible known as Matthew, Mark, Luke and John. These books record the life of Jesus on earth. Same story, different writers' perspectives.

Please record the perspective God has given you, or the greatest impact He has brought your heart today through the study of His Word.

_____

_____

_____

_____

Thank you muchly~

Day 2: Who He Is

Hi! Picking up right where we left off yesterday let us glance at the very beginning of each gospel to get a sense of their purpose. Going in order we will start with Matthew.

God honors those who honor Him (1 Sam. 2:30) so let us be sure to begin in prayer honoring our God as Leader in this study.

Please read Matthew 1:1-17 and please note the only four women listed in that genealogical record.

_____

_____

Verse 3 - Tamar: slept with her father in law. (Gen. 38)

Verse 5 - Rahab: a woman in the business of prostitution. (Josh. 2)

Verse 5 - Ruth: a pagan gal. (Ruth 1-4)

Verse 6 - Bathsheba: committed adultery. (2 Sam. 11)

God wanted, loved and transformed with Truth what most of the world would have thrown away.

Are we allowing that very same God to work that very same transforming Truth into and over our own lives?

Please fill in the blanks according to 1 Samuel 16:7 (ESV) below.
...For the LORD sees _____ _as man sees: man looks on the_ _____
appearance, but the LORD looks on the _____.”_
(not, outward, heart)

The world is good at posing perfection, you don't have to scroll very far on social media to find it. But our God who sees past the posing isn't looking for perfect people. Rather people perfectly devoted to Him despite their imperfections.

Romans 7:18 (NIV) states, *For I know that good itself does not dwell in me, that is, in my sinful nature. For I have the desire to do what is good, but I cannot carry it out.*

What does Matthew 15:18-19 and Jeremiah 17:9 tell us about our hearts and what is the question asked in Jeremiah?

_____

_____

Who can understand it?!

In our quest for Truth seek the One who knit our hearts together, who knows us better than we know ourselves and loves us even still! LOVES US EVEN STILL! Loves us just as we are, and enough to take us beyond what we ever thought we could be!

Record Psalm 139:23-24 and Psalm 51:10 as a prayer to keep us from wayward hearts.

_____

_____

May we not quench His Spirit but allow Him ever increasing space within us. For true beauty, lasting beauty (no creams required) comes from within.

After Matthew comes Mark and we will pick that book up soon however for right now please skip to Luke.

Luke 1:3-4 (NLT) *Having carefully investigated everything from the beginning, I also have decided to write a careful account for you, most honorable Theophilus, so you can be certain of the truth of everything you were taught.*

Please circle "certain of the truth" in the above verse. Pretty clear purpose for writing!

Please circle "Theophilus" in Luke 1:3-4 above. "Theophilus means 'loved by God'"[iv] so I think it is safe to say it's written to all of us in order to … ? (We just stated it above.)

_____

We are all so loved by God that He wants us to <u>be certain of the Truth</u>!

Please see Luke 3:23 and record the age of Jesus when He began His earthly ministry. _____ It is never too late to get started dear one on the path and plan He has purposed for your life! *Just in case 30 seems young… Caleb was 40, Moses was 80, Sarah was 90, Abraham was 100, Noah was 600… when God chose them to step up in His master plan!

Young, old, prime time is really God's time! Numbers 14:24 (NLT) states, *But my servant Caleb has a different attitude than the others have.* May we all pray to have some of that different attitude than that which conforms to the rest of the world. We want to be as willing as Isaiah and as eager as Caleb, always, in season and out of season (2 Tim. 4:2)!!

Please record below Isaiah's response to God in Isaiah 6:8.

_____

Joshua 14:10-12 records that Caleb, even at 85 years old, was still full of vigor and energy for the Lord, asking Him to bring on the next mountain with the giants!

Here am I, send me! Bring on the next mountain Lord! Is something we proclaim with confidence the more deeply we know our God because the more we know Him the more we know His trustworthy and faithful character. He has more strength, ability, ideas, mercy and grace then we could ever fathom! He is the great I AM of Exodus 3:14! We may not know or understand our circumstance, but we can always know and trust His faithful presence with us. We are never alone!

Our last gospel book is John, and we are right back where we started our day yesterday! Our weeks beginning verse is John 20:31 and it gives us our purpose. Please briefly record your purpose for pursuing this study.

Who in John 1:6 is sent to tell about the Light of Jesus coming?

Please fill in the blank according to John 1:7 (NLT).

to tell about the light so that everyone might _____ *because of his testimony.*
(believe)

Who might God be trying to reach through you? Who is in your circle of influence?

As a believer you have the Light of Jesus inside you and what does John 1:5 tell us about that Light?

The darkness CAN NOT overcome it! It CAN NOT be extinguished!!

Please record 2 Corinthians 2:14 and just hover over the word "triumphal" and let the meaning of it sink into your core! As I have been reminded, we don't fight for victory but from it dear one!

As we study over these next few weeks may God remind us of what we learned over these past two days…

- He wants EVERYONE (YOU) to believe in Him and receive eternal life.

- Remember you are dearly loved by Him and He desires for us to be certain of the Truth.

- He has given us great purpose with each gift of breath no matter our age in spreading His victorious Light to the world.

- He is with us… why? …because that is just Who He is! In closing please fill in the blank below according to Matthew 1:23 (NIV).

"The virgin will conceive and give birth to a son, and they will call him _____ *" (which means "*_____ _____ _____*").*
(Immanuel – God with us)

Thank you sincerely, dear one, for today! God bless you muchly~

Before leaving please spend a moment in prayer with God and record below what God highlighted for your heart especially from today's study.

_____
_____
_____
_____

Day 3: Float on Hope

Welcome back! It is so good to have you here again and knowing that God Almighty is with us too just makes a heart quiver with delight does it not!?!! Let us bow and thank Him for His presence but also surrender to His leading as we drink in the Living Water of His Word. *Then the way you live will always honor and please the Lord, and your lives will produce every kind of good fruit. All the while, you will grow as you learn to know God better and better. We also pray that you will be strengthened with all his glorious power so you will have all the endurance and patience you need. May you be filled with joy, always thanking the Father. He has enabled you to share in the inheritance that belongs to his people, who live in the light. For he has rescued us from the kingdom of darkness and transferred us into the Kingdom of his dear Son, who purchased our freedom and forgave our sins.* Colossians 1:10-14 (NLT) Well now THAT is a Scripture to kick off a day of study! Let us begin dear one.

Something to tuck into the pocket of your heart today: *"How kind the LORD is!" she exclaimed. "He has taken away my disgrace…"* (Luke 1:25 NLT)

Please read Luke 1:5-25 and just savor this story as if you were right there on location! Go ahead and check here when you have completed it. _____

According to verses 5-6 who are Zechariah and Elizabeth?
_____

Good people from good people however what is the heart ache or impossible situation that they have always had to deal with stated in verse 7?
_____

We often want to equate obedience to God with success. Even without realizing it we can sometimes become offended by God or some human because of an entitled attitude we did not even know we had! We subconsciously have kept track of all the good we have done, all we feel we have sacrificed for God or another and then all of a sudden when that person or God doesn't give back or respond to a certain situation in such a way we feel they should or we are owed, we become hurt, angry, bitter, resentful, revengeful, stubborn… you name it and it's probably been done, thought or felt under the sun!

Can you recall a time you thought you were trusting God, but it turned out you were only trusting in something you felt entitled to? I we more spoiled or trusting?
_____
_____

Please hold your spot in Luke as we turn for a moment and read Acts chapter 5:17-42, it is just a WILD string of events!! _____
Did you check the line when finished? I don't know about you, but I find checking something off quite satisfying! (Don't tell anyone but I will actually add something to my "to-do" list if I have finished something during the day that was not originally there just to feel the satisfaction of time recorded well spent!)

Things in life rarely come in neat little checked boxes and I think the longer we live the more we are glad that they do not. A beautiful mess is the sign of a WILD adventure! We only get one life, one adventure to live and God knew if we lived it full out, we were going to need second chances. Praise Him, each new day is a second chance!

In Acts these men are given second chances and each time they use them for God's glory! What happens to the apostles because of other people's jealousy in verses 17-18?

_____

What happens in the very next verse (Acts 5:19)?

_____

Ironic is it not, that Sadducees did not believe angels existed! (See Acts 23:8) That is why they are sad-u-see. (Ha-ha, couldn't help that one!)

They are told to do what in Acts 5:20?

_____

They were just thrown in jail for this so what do they do with their second chance once set free (verse 21)?

_____

WOW right!

They choose to be faithfully obedient because we are set free to set others free (Luke 22:32) and what happens in verse Acts 5:26?

_____

What a difference between a believer and an unbeliever. Acts 5:26 records the captain and the temple guards all afraid of the people, yet these mere disciples have no fear of the people (verse 29) because they bow to a higher power, God Most High.

Instead of becoming angry with God that they were again imprisoned following their obedience, what do they say in verse 29?

_____

They see this as an opportunity to bring the Good News, to point the people's attention back to Jesus! I find it interesting that the first question the guards and people ask them is not, how in the world did you escape prison but rather why did you not obey us (verse 28)?! A refocus on Truth was truly needed!

How have you been able to use a situation that seemed at first less than desirable
as a magnifying glass for Truth?

_____

_____

Now surely, they have endured hardship enough and remained faithful so things must take a turn for the better! Yet what happens in Acts 5:33?

_____

When the people should have been set free by the Truth, they chose to become furious instead. What does Matthew 10:14 advise us to do in such situations?

_____

Sometimes after you have done all you can, you need to shake the dust off and keep moving forward - it is the only direction faith faces.

By Acts 5:40 the apostles are FLOGGED! Good golly they can't seem to catch a break and yet what is their response in verses 41 and 42?!!!

_____

How? Why? I believe they were aware of the incomprehensible suffering their Savior Jesus Christ had endured on their behalf - on our behalf - and it felt like an honor to be counted worthy to suffer for Him, a small token of gratitude to offer back to God for paying a debt we never could have! He suffered so we could live eternally! If we get nothing else on this side of heaven, eternal salvation is enough! He has saved us so that our world does not end in a pool of tears, heartache and floggings!

Please summarize and record below what stands out the most to you in 1 Corinthians 2:9 and Revelation 21:4 regarding what He has saved us to.

_____

_____

_____

In Genesis 3 we brought suffering into our world however John 16:33 (NIV) tells us, *"I have told you these things, so that in me you may have peace. In this world you will have trouble. But take heart! I have overcome the world."* Matthew 24:13 (NIV) *but the one who stands firm to the end will be saved.* Romans 8:31 (NIV) *What, then, shall we say in response to these things? If God is for us, who can be against us?* So, Psalm 130:5 (NIV) *I wait for the LORD, my whole being waits, and in his word I put my hope.*

Notice that the last word in Psalm 130:5 is not cope. His Word makes it clear we were made for more than coping through! We were made for hoping! Hoping with a hope that will not disappoint (Romans 5:5)! In His Word we can put our HOPE. Living hope moves us beyond a life that just cope's! John 10:10 said He came to give us abundant life! Abundant goes beyond coping, way beyond!

Back to Luke 1. We see Zechariah and Elizabeth do just this, hope in His Word. How have you put your hope in His Word? What verses or passages of Scripture hold you steadfast when the waves of the unknown or discouragement threaten to capsize your lifeboat?

_____

I wonder if there is someone in your circle of influence that could use one of these "floatation devices" of yours? If you need one, here are some of mine Romans 8:37 or Philippians 4:13 or Romans 15:13 or Isaiah 26:3, 41:13, and Psalm 32:8.

Dear one you were made to float on a sure hope! Take time to record what God used to make the greatest impact on your heart today as you spent time with Him. See you tomorrow!

_____
_____
_____
_____

Day 4: Who Not How

Welcome back!! We will jump in right where we left off but first let us pray that God would still all the distractions that would pull our hearts from His at this time.

Remember we were studying Luke 1:5-25. If you need to first briefly skim over that passage once more to regain our focus for today go right ahead!
Zechariah and Elizabeth were still found walking faithful through all the disappointment they had experienced. What happens in Luke 1:11?

_____

Where is Zechariah exactly when this occurs (verse 11)?

_____

Please read Psalm 73. _____

In all that is not understood when do things become clear? (Hint: verse 17) Please record Psalm 73:17 below.

_____

_____

In the sanctuary of God was it remembered that this is not our home but that the tapestry God is weaving is just so very much bigger and more beautiful than we could comprehend! What advice does Romans 12:2 give us?

_____

_____

Please record Zechariah's question stated in Luke 1:18 below.

_____

Have you ever had a "How?" question for our Lord?   Circle: YES   NO

Romans 11:33-36 (NLT) *Oh, how great are God's riches and wisdom and knowledge! How impossible it is for us to understand his decisions and his ways! For who can know the LORD's thoughts? Who knows enough to give him advice? And who has given him so much that he needs to pay it back? For everything comes from him and exists by his power and is intended for his glory. All glory to him forever! Amen.*

Oh, how impossible it is for us, the created, to understand the mind of the Creator. So rather than try to figure out the un-figured-out-able may we put our energies into developing a relationship with our good Creator God who so very much wants to be near us.

1 Corinthians 2:16 (NLT) *For, "Who can know the LORD's thoughts? Who knows enough to teach him? But we understand these things, for we have the mind of Christ.* God's divine wisdom obviously transcends all human reasoning however with His Holy Spirit within us He can reveal the mind of Christ to us!

Knowing WHO may not explain all our "how's" out for our current understanding; instead the One who knows best promises a peace that passes our understanding in all we don't yet know will be ours if we know and trust the One who does. As we close please read John 14:1, 27.

As we embark further on our quest may God always remind us of treasures, we have gathered with Him.

- Do not allow the attitude of entitlement to keep you from fully experiencing the adventure of an authentic, trusting relationship with our loving Creator God.

- In all we do not know continue to run TO Him. It is in His presence, His sanctuary that we will find clarity of focus.

- Prayerfully let all your "how's?" rest in the mighty hand of Who you know is all knowing and good. *And the peace of God, which transcends all understanding, will guard your hearts and your minds in Christ Jesus.* Philippians 4:7 (NIV)

For, *"How kind the Lord is!" she exclaimed. "He has taken away my disgrace…"* Luke 1:25 (NLT) Oh how He has dear one, oh how He has! *God made him who had no sin to be sin for us, so that in him we might become the righteousness of God.* 2 Corinthians 5:21 (NIV) I do not know HOW it all works but I do know WHO makes it all work and that is enough for now. *For now we see only a reflection as in a mirror; then we shall see face to face. Now I know in part; then I shall know fully, even as I am fully known.* 1 Corinthians 13:12 (NIV) So, *I wait for the LORD, my whole being waits, and in his word I put my hope.* Psalm 130:5 (NIV) *Let us hold unswervingly to the hope we profess, for he who promised is faithful.* Hebrews 10:23 (NIV)

He WHO promised is faithful! Praise Him! Thank you for today~
Before leaving please spend a moment in prayer with God and record below
what God highlighted for your heart especially from today's study.

_____

_____

_____

_____

Day 5: Plan or Purpose

Hi! I just came back from taking our dog for a walk. His name is Brave and is
the largest British Lab quite possibly God has ever made! When we take him
for a walk, the word "walk" is only a relative term for what really takes place.
We purpose a walk, Brave plans to experience every single smell from every
living thing as if it will self-destruct if he does not get to it on time! He pulls
like a sled dog at full speed bounding from one living thing to another, panting
and grunting, slobber flying… our horse sized dog has no shame, none. For
safety's sake it is both hands on leash at all times (unless you start dragging
behind on your stomach then just release the hound, he'll be back as soon as
you cook up some bacon!)
It will now take Brave the better part of the next hour to slow his ragged
panting from the excitement of his "walk". If only he would just follow our
purpose to enjoy each other's company and take in the sights and smells as we
go, he would save himself the humiliating agony and physical strain he puts
himself through! I wonder how often our God purposes a walk with us and
due to our own "plan" we are too caught up in, we lose the joy of it all
together?!! Let us begin in prayer that God's higher and better purpose in our
study today would prevail through all our seemingly well laid plans.

Tuck in your hearts pocket Brave's namesake verse: *Be strong and courageous. Do
not be afraid or terrified because of them, for the Lord your God goes with you; he will never
leave you nor forsake you."* Deuteronomy 31:6 (NIV)

Please begin by reading Luke 1:26-56. _____

We left off yesterday with Elizabeth becoming pregnant. Today we pick up six
months into her pregnancy when the same angel that appeared to Zechariah

(Luke 1:19) now appears to a young gal named Mary (Luke 1:26). What message does the angel Gabriel have for young Mary? (Hint: Luke 1:31-33)

_____

_____

Remember that Gabriel was the same angel that also appeared to Zechariah. In fact, Gabriel is the same angel that appears to Daniel hundreds of years earlier! (See Daniel 8:15-17) If you want to see something wild just detour with me for a moment to Daniel 9:20-23. ____
There is a whole spiritual world out there we cannot see with our physical eyes and prayer my dear child is more deeply POWERFUL then I think anyone of us can comprehend!

So here we are with our timeless angel Gabriel again in today's Scripture… (What encouragement that our God *is the same yesterday and today and forever* (Heb. 13:8).) The same God with Daniel was the same God with Mary and is the same God that stands with you today!

Now hold up, just wait one minute!!! Luke 1:27 indicates Mary ALREADY had some well laid plans of her own!! What were they?

_____

Any newly engaged people out there ready to chuck it all on one angel encounter?! Luke 1:29 indicates Mary probably felt the same way at first… NLT puts it that she was, *confused and disturbed*, NIV puts it that she was, *greatly troubled*. No matter which way you read it she was not leaping with ecstatic joy to be placing all her plans on… well not even on stand-by but rather laying them down in order to embrace a completely different and higher purpose beyond her wildest imagination OR comprehension!!!

Mary does ask the angel a question in verse 34. What is it?

_____

At first glance this seems remarkably like Zechariah's question in Luke 1:18 but unlike Zechariah Mary does not lose her voice over the whole thing. Why not? I think the answer lies in Matthew 18:3. What does this verse tell us we are to be like in our faith?

To clarify: Child-LIKE not child-ISH faith.

Why do you think we are to have child-like faith?

_____

Have you ever taken a small child on a walk? You end up with your pockets FULL of acorn tops, feathers, leaves and "special" rocks... (Just to name a few of the treasures you are asked to keep safe until you get home.) Somewhere between childhood and adulthood sadly we lose some of that wonder for all things miraculous! Like acorn tops that fit so perfectly on the ends of your fingertips!

I think Zechariah's question of "How…?" came from a heart of doubting it was even possible, all things considered. But Mary... Mary's question I believe came from a heart of wonder! "Oh, how wonder-FULL Lord! I don't know 'how' You are going to do this thing but once again You have stolen my heart with wonder!"

When was the last time you let Him steal your heart afresh with childlike wonder? Today's challenge is to take a walk or sit outside for a moment and ask God to steal your breath away with the sheer beauty of His wonder. Record below your experience if you like.

_____
_____
_____

Matthew 13:16 (NIV) *But blessed are your eyes because they see, and your ears because they hear.*

Thank you muchly for today dear one. Take a moment to reflect with God on what you have studied today.

_____
_____
_____
_____

Day 6 & 7: At His Feet – A Time to Reflect

Over the next two days take time to reflect over your week of study. Maybe you need some time to catch up on the study material and this might be the perfect break to do just that with the Lord!

I encourage you to glance back at the final point at the end of each day that you recorded having had the greatest impact on your heart. As you spend time with God in prayer, reflect and record on the lines below how God is tying it together and applying it to your life specifically for such a time as this.

Ask that God make it clear who He would have you invite into a natural opportunity to share Him, to apply what you are learning; maybe a child, grandchild, friend… trust Him to continue to take the lead. May we have a heart ever ready with eyes and ears out to the opportunities God wants to invite us into for His glory and praise.

Do not merely listen to the word, and so deceive yourselves. Do what it says. Anyone who listens to the word but does not do what it says is like someone who looks at his face in a mirror and, after looking at himself, goes away and immediately forgets what he looks like. But whoever looks intently into the perfect law that gives freedom, and continues in it – not forgetting what they have heard, but doing it – they will be blessed in what they do. James 1:22-25 (NIV)

_____
_____
_____
_____
_____
_____
_____
_____
_____
_____

Philippians 4:13 (NIV) *I can do all this through him who gives me strength.*

John 14:26 (NIV) *But the Advocate, the Holy Spirit, whom the Father will send in my name, will teach you all things and will remind you of everything I have said to you.*

WEEK 2
All who heard him were amazed at his understanding and his answers.
Luke 2:47 (NLT)

Day 1: Overshadowed
Hi! Thank you sincerely for the tenacity you have shown in your study this past week and for the endurance to continue this week. Let us ensure a strong start by beginning in prayer that God Almighty lead and help us follow.

We will pick up right where we left off yesterday in Luke. If needed go ahead and briefly skim Luke 1:26-56 for a brain refresher.

What explanation does the angel respond to Mary with, in Luke 1:35?

_____

...the power of the Most High will overshadow you... (Luke 1:35 NLT)

I wonder if this created an image in Mary's mind like it did mine from the Old Testament Scriptures? Psalm 91:4 paints a vivid and comforting picture for me on what it looks like to be overshadowed by our Most High God. Record below what it is about Psalm 91:4 (printed below) that brings comfort to your heart.

Psalm 91:4 (NLT) *He will cover you with his feathers. He will shelter you with his wings. His faithful promises are your armor and protection.*

Verse impact:

_____

_____

If this is the aftertaste of being in God's shadow, so to speak, what is the aftertaste of your shadow? Let us first look at Acts 5:12-16.

What happened to people that fell in Peter's shadow?

_____

They were healed, not by his shadow but by the power of the Holy Spirit within him. This pointed to the power of God!

Is your life casting a shadow that glows for Him? Does the aftertaste of your life leave people craving more of Him? We can all pray that with each new day of second chances our shadow glows ever more brightly. So bright we reflect Him more clearly so that others are left craving Him of which there is an endless supply for eternity! Amen!

Back to our story in Luke chapter 1 and we see that Mary responds to all that she had NOT planned for her life, with what, in verse 38?

_____

She was willing to surrender her will and plans to His higher purpose. Already her "shadow" glows with a reflection of Him. Matthew 26:36-46 records Jesus just before His crucifixion surrendering His will to the Father's. Jesus took a "no" for a greater purposed "yes" a "yes" that would be for us. All of us who choose to believe in His sacrifice in our place, now have the Way to eternal life (John 14:6)!

In God's great kindness He provided Elizabeth for young Mary. Luke 1:39 indicates Mary hurried off to visit her! Who has God in His kindness provided you with as an encouragement in the faith? Have you thanked God for that person? Have you thanked them lately or let them know how much they mean to you? Ask God how you might give back to them this week.

_____

_____

Proverbs 11:25 (NIV) *A generous person will prosper; whoever refreshes others will be refreshed.*

How long is Mary recorded having spent visiting her friend? (See Luke 1:56)

_____

What might happen for you within 90 days spent in fellowship with other believers? *And let us not neglect our meeting together, as some people do, but encourage one another, especially now that the day of his return is drawing near.* Hebrews 10:25 (NLT)

Mary's response to the angel and according to her song of praise in verses 46-55 clearly indicates that her life's goal was not to live out her plan but to fulfill His greater purpose.

Mary knew her God. In Exodus 3:14 God gives us the name "I AM" for Himself. There is nothing He cannot be to, and for you, at any time. He is the great I AM!

Mary chose to trust His overshadowing and was willing to surrender to His faithful provision to be all that she would ever need that she did not yet even know to ask for! Mary was able to let go of her good plan to embrace His better purpose for her life. The God who enraptured her heart with breathless wonder did not have to wonder where she stood. *Mary responded, "I am the Lord's servant. May everything you have said about me come true."* (Luke 1:38 NLT)

Can you insert your name for Mary's in the above verse? Might we pray to be able to, whatever the cost.

Matthew 10:39 (NIV) *Whoever finds their life will lose it, and whoever loses their life for my sake will find it.* James 4:14 reminds us that this life is but a vapor a mist here today and gone tomorrow compared to eternity. Considering this Truth how will we live today… for our plans or for His Kingdom purpose? He leaves the choice up to us; oh, that our shadows would leave a sweet aftertaste for future generations to crave Truth!

Before we sign off let us review a few important points we can all pray over gathered throughout our study so far…

- Pray for a wonder-FULL childlike faith.

- Pray for an attitude of humble surrender that He might replace our finite minded plans for His Kingdom minded purposes.

- Pray for a shadow that glows of Him.

- Pray for ever increasing trust in the great I AM.

Blessed is she who has believed that the Lord would fulfill his promises to her!" Luke 1:45 (NIV)

You have blessed me with your presence today. Thank you sincerely~
Before leaving please spend a moment in prayer with God and record below
what God highlighted for your heart from today's study.

_____

_____

_____

_____

Day 2: Praise and Perspective

Greetings beloved child of God! From where you are sitting what is your
perspective? Not to be too deep, mine is a wall. A wall wallpapered with sticky
notes filled with wisdom way beyond my own! You know it was said
somewhere that it really is not about whether your glass is half full or half
empty, it's that your glass is refillable. By golly just having a glass is something
to be grateful for! How's that for some fresh perspective!?!!

Revelation 22:17 in the NIV tells us, *The Spirit and the bride say, "Come!" And let
the one who hears say, "Come!" Let the one who is thirsty come; and let the one who wishes
take the free gift of the water of life.*

Let us begin our day in prayer just praising our God that we have a "glass" and
in Him our "glass" is refillable! May He always lead us into His greater
purpose through His greater perspective.

To tuck into your heart's pocket: *From his abundance we have all received one gracious
blessing after another.* John 1:16 (NLT)

Please read Luke 1:57-80, giving perspective on today's study. _____

Today we begin with the exciting birth of Zechariah and Elizabeth's baby boy,
John the Baptist!!! Verse 57 encompasses that whole miraculous event in one
simple sentence, *When it was time for Elizabeth's baby to be born, she gave birth to a
son.* Luke 1:57 (NLT) Now, I have given birth to six babies and let me tell you
I would need way more than one sentence to describe each and every one of
them!!! However, the birth process was not the focus here, it was what was
birthed.

What God is working out of us is going to far outweigh the pains of and in the process. 2 Corinthians 4:17 (NIV) tells us, *For our light and momentary troubles are achieving for us an eternal glory that far outweighs them all.*

You might be thinking that your present troubles are anything but light and momentary however, while giving birth naturally, neither did I, but what was birthed forth afterward truly did in every way outweigh all the pain in the process!

In Luke 1:58 everyone rejoiced with Elizabeth when they had heard what?

_____

They rejoiced upon hearing of the Lord's great mercy.

It just is not easy or comfortable to be in a place requiring mercy is it? Mercy means kindness is shown instead of punishment. When it would be in someone's power to administer harm, compassion is shown in its place. How quick are we to join in rejoicing with another rather than judge someone that has received mercy from the Lord? Is there anyone in your circle of influence that you have the power to show mercy toward? Is there anyone you know that has received mercy from the Lord that you could rejoice with?

_____

_____

Matthew 18:21-22 (NIV) *Then Peter came to Jesus and asked, "Lord, how many times shall I forgive my brother or sister who sins against me? Up to seven times?" Jesus answered, "I tell you, not seven times, but seventy-seven times.*

In Luke 1:60 Elizabeth steps forward in obedience, naming her son what God has commanded and what is the response from the crowd? (See verse 61)

_____

WHAT?!??

Then in verse 63 Zechariah has now come to believe God is indeed capable of the impossible and against all that would seem logical to name their son he obeys God's command as well to name their baby boy John.

It was not until Zechariah took hold of his second chance and wrote down on the tablet the name God gave his son, that his voice opened. Dear one, it is when we finally submit to God writing HIS story on the tablet of our minds and hearts that we too will find our true self open.

What did this couple's obedience lead to the crowds of people pondering over in verse 66?

_____

_____

"What will this child turn out to be?" For the hand of the Lord was surely upon him in a special way. (Luke 1:66 NLT)

People may question what you do, why you do it… for example why save sex for marriage alone? (See Hebrews 13:4) But may all their questions and pondering over why you do what you do, why you speak like you speak, all point them to the God you follow. May they all point to the fact that God's almighty hand is on your life and in order for you not to miss out on any of the special plans God has for you, you choose to make choices that will honor Him with the gift of life He's given you.

God only wants the absolute best possible for you. John 10:10 (NIV) *The thief comes only to steal and kill and destroy; I have come that they may have life, and have it to the full.*

Do NOT believe the enemy's lies that if you have fallen short, you are out. Each new day is a second chance to begin again!

Read the following verses on this subject and record the encouragement you receive from the Truth.

Romans 3:23 ____
Micah 7:8 ____
Lamentations 3:22-23 ____
2 Corinthians 5:17 ____
Psalm 103:12 ____

_____

_____

_____

Oh, dear one, I pray the Truth rings louder in your head and heart than the lies of the enemy!

What a perspective shift Zechariah has made in the last nine months during his "Holy Hush" as I have heard it called. Like Mary in Luke 1:46-55, in Luke 1:67-79 we read Zechariah was given a new song of praise in his heart! Not because it all made sense and had become clear but because a decision was made to trust, to make a faith step in God's direction, to obey BEFORE all the questions were answered because the perspective of Who God was/is/will be, had become, I AM is enough!

What area(s) in your life might you need a perspective shift to see God as I AM enough in all things? He is not a God that wants to be compartmentalized.

_____

_____

In Luke 1:76 (NLT) Zechariah speaks words of life over his son that were first spoken by our God. *"And you, my little son, will be called the prophet of the Most High because you will prepare the way for the Lord.*

Do we speak words of life over the lives in our sphere of influence? Do we proclaim over them, about them, that which God would? Do we see the butterfly God is developing them into or do we only dwell on their cocoon?

As we close today and record what God has impacted us the most with, let us pray for eyes that see like God does as we praise Him for seeing US with His eyes of unfailing love, mercy and grace.

_____

_____

_____

_____

Day 3: The Great I AM

Greetings dear one. Before we continue our study from yesterday let us pray that the same God yesterday, today and forever (Heb. 13:8) will faithfully lead us deeper into His heart today.

Please read John 1:1-18. _____

Can you see the correlation between what was spoken over John the Baptist as a baby and what is recorded about his life by John, Jesus' disciple? List some of what you compared below. (Hint: John 1:5-9 and Luke 1:76-79)

_____

_____

As great as John the Baptist was, he never lost perspective on his purpose and just Who was greater. John's life mission was to sing the praises of the coming Messiah, to prepare the way for Him. Do you see a comparison between the mission of John the Baptist's life and your own?

_____

_____

We are all called to sing the praises of our God as we prepare for His promised return!

Praise is so often the key to proper perspective. What is your baseline for praise? Before you answer that read Psalm 150:6.

It was pointed out to me once that that verse does NOT say everything that is financially stable, praise, or everything that is healthy, praise, or everything that has perfect circumstances, praise. Psalm 150:6 (NIV) tells me, *Let everything that has breath praise the LORD. Praise the LORD.*

So, the baseline for praising the Lord is if we have a breath! What do you praise Him for right now?

_____

_____

_____

_____

Praise Him that...
He is I AM... able to work all things for good. (Romans 8:28)
He is I AM... with you always. (Joshua 1:9)
He is I AM... your best planner. (Jeremiah 29:11)
He is I AM... your provision. (Phil. 4:19)
He is I AM... your living Hope. (1 Peter 1:3)

He is I AM… your love. (1 John 4:8)
…and I am only getting started!

Luke 1:80 (NLT) begins with, *John grew up and became strong in spirit.* This is my prayer for all of us as we continue our trek through this Bible study together.

Some points that have added strength to my spirit from our study and hopefully to yours as well...

- Mercy is something to rejoice over and to give freely away to others as we have so freely been given. (Matthew 10:8)

- Let those who ponder or question the way you live be turned to notice the mighty hand of God on your life.

- Speak life over those in your sphere of influence.

- Let your praise transform your perspective to His.

God bless you muchly~

Before leaving please spend a moment in prayer with God and record below what God highlighted for your heart especially from today's study.

_____
_____
_____
_____

Day 4: Go with God

Welcome back! I pray opportunity has come your way to savor sharing with someone a few of the sweet Truth's God has been working into your heart lately.

Please bow before Him with me asking that He lead and write out His lesson on hearts offered up as willing tablets in His hands.

Please read Matthew 1:18-25. _____

How does Mathew 1:19 describe Joseph?

_____

And what has he decided to do?

_____

What happens as he is considering this (vs. 20)?

_____

Have you ever been in a similar spot as Joseph? You are trying to make a good decision, but things seem more grey then black and white. There just seems to be no easy way. So, you kind of have your mind made up but still your heart is being tugged as you contemplate just how you will go about things correctly?! Care to share your example below?

_____

_____

_____

Hebrews 11:6 (NIV) *And without faith it is impossible to please God, because anyone who comes to him must believe that he exists and that he rewards those who earnestly seek him.*

He wants to be found by us and He desires for us to do His will so He will not keep it hidden but our walk with Him will require faith. When we are wrestling with a decision, pray! Pray for pure motives and His purpose and wisdom to prevail. Seek wise counsel and match up their advice with His Word. Read His Word as you pray and seek His heart on the matter. If your answer is not crystal clear at the time you need to decide, then you make a decision the best you know how and trust that IF you have stepped wrong God is big enough to trump your mistake.

Please read the following verses and record the one that resonates with your heart the most on the lines below.

Isaiah 30:21 ____
Proverbs 3:5-6 ____
Psalm 32:8 ____
Proverbs 16:9 ____

_____

_____

Joseph, though he thought he knew what to do did not jump in haste. Joseph took time to wait and consider things a bit and while he did so, it gave God time to intervene.

In all that Joseph thought he understood he allowed God time to instruct him in all he misunderstood. What happens in Matthew 1:20?

_____

_____

How humble is our heart to wait on God, to ask God's advice when we already think we know it all?

_____

What advice does Psalm 27:14 and Isaiah 30:18 along with 1 Peter 5:6-8 give us?

_____

_____

_____

The sequence in 1 Peter 5:6-8 is so divine! Humility is mentioned first in verse 5… however choosing the humble way can cause a bit of anxiety if you really think about it… so verse 7 right away tells us to cast that ball of anxiety in His court! Why? Because verse 8 tells us the enemy is prowling around just waiting to seep through all the prideful anxiety ridden cracks of our mind and heart!

What does Matthew 1:24 tell us Joseph does?

_____

WOW, right?!! I mean can you just imagine all the questions he could have had for God when he woke up?!!! Instead Joseph obeys God's Word without hesitation! During all he may not have understood, or thought did not line up, or even amid frustration and resentment, Joseph humbled himself under God's mighty hand. Joseph chose to hand God the ball of anxiety probably threatening to rest right on top of his lungs and God was honored through his faithful obedience.

AS Joseph walked out his faith (not before) God proved faithful and to be, I AM with you every step of the way as we will see as we study further! However, I believe that it was in all the ways that God HAD proved faithful within Joseph's past, that emboldened his faith to step forward into the unknown because what was known was with Whom he went with.

Fill in the following blanks according to John 14:15 (ESV) below.
"If you _____ me, you will keep my _____.
(love, commandments)

As we finish for today let's pray that God continue to make Himself known to us. That He give us eyes and ears to perceive His presence in our today's as He reminds and reveals His faithfulness in all our yesterday's. I'm praying that as we study His heart we allow Him to develop us into people that bring ALL things before our all mighty, all knowing, ever present God; the things we think we know and the things we don't. Why? Because we trust Him in/with all things.

Dear one, let us reverence and honor His way above our own as we go with God. Please record the point of greatest impact to your heart today.

_____
_____
_____
_____

Your fingers did a lot of miles traveling through His Word today! Great study! Thank you!!

Day 5: Let Go and Let's Go

Welcome dear one, begin in prayer and then let us focus our attention on our Scripture today found in Luke 2:1-20 _____

Who is the Roman emperor currently (Luke 2:1)? _____

Luke's predominantly Greek audience would have been interested in such history and political recordings. The Roman rulers were like gods to people at that time and could not have been more different in comparison to the tiny baby in a manger who was truly God in the flesh. (*Life Application Study Bible* notes, pg. 1889)

Augustus's decree went out in God's perfect timing and according to God's perfect plan.

We see God can use ANYONE to work through and bring about His perfect plan.

Job 42:2 (NIV) ends, *no purpose of yours can be thwarted.*

How willing are you to learn from ANYONE God brings across your path?

_____

We can learn from anyone, whether it's how to be or how NOT to be, we can learn if we are open.

God was using Augustus's decree to work out His plan to bring His Son to the right place at the right time. Looking at Luke 2:5-7 how well do you think Joseph and Mary saw God's plan falling together?!

_____

_____

Who wants to travel when they are OBVIOUSLY extremely close to giving birth?! "This can't be God's timing Joseph!" I imagine Mary exclaiming when Joe brings home the news that they had to travel. Then they arrive after some three days by foot and donkey and there is NO place available! "SEE Joe, I told you this was NOT God's way!" I imagine Mary exclaiming.

I am sure Mary had a much humbler approach than I, but how quick are we to give up or give in when our circumstances are not aligning just so?

_____

_____

It WAS God's way to have His Son Jesus, the Savior of the world be born in a humble manger. Mark 10:45 (NIV) *For even the Son of Man did not come to be served, but to serve, and to give his life as a ransom for many."*

Now we come to the shepherds in our saga. Again, we see God doing things in the way we would least expect. Of all the people God could have brought the news to first it was lowly shepherds. I wonder if any of these shepherds supplied the lambs for the sacrifices at the Temple for the forgiveness of sin? Now the angels were inviting them to be the first to witness and worship the Lamb of God that would take away the sins of the whole world!

Reading Luke 2:8-14 what would your response have been if you had been one of the shepherds?

_____

_____

Like Joseph I can imagine they were awestruck beyond comprehension and could have insisted on asking so many questions or, asked for further proof. They could have let fear overtake them and not move at all but what in fact do they exclaim as soon as the angels leave them in Luke 2:15?

_____

LET'S GO!!!

Might we pray for a heart of "LET'S GO!" when we know God has spoken and asked us to come see. "Come see." does not give a whole lot of details but indicates a whole lot of trust will be needed. How does trust grow? Like in any relationship, it grows over time, it grows one step at a time. The more time you spend with God, choosing to be obedient will give trust a chance to grow so we can let go and just go as He proves Himself faithful with each step.

Please fill in the blanks below according to 2 Timothy 2:13 (NIV).
If we are _____, he remains _____, for he cannot disown himself. (faithless, faithful)

Did the shepherds find things just as the angels had said (Luke 2:20)?
YES   or   NO

What do the shepherds do in Luke 2:20?

_____

Glorify and praise God! They had experienced God's faithfulness and were overflowing with joy!

How have you experienced God's faithfulness in such a way that you have been filled with joy? How have you praised and glorified Him for it?

_____
_____
_____
_____

Psalm 107:1-3 (NIV) *Give thanks to the LORD, for he is good; his love endures forever. Let the redeemed of the LORD tell their story-- those he redeemed from the hand of the foe, those he gathered from the lands, from the east and west, from north and south.*

We have studied Joseph's willingness to consider God, and in all that he had already decided, Joseph allowed God to trump his plans and follow willingly in trust.

We have studied how Mary could have made or at least validated every excuse under the sun for stopping in her tracks due to how untimely and inconvenient her circumstances appeared rather than continue forward as she did in her God.

We have studied how the shepherds could have doubted and in fear chose to stay put on those hills but instead found God faithful in every way as they were willing to "go and see!".
Sometimes in order to find God's way we just need to get out of the way! Sometimes we are our own biggest stumbling block! Will we ride the boat of belief or doubt in our storm? The choice is ours. Please record what you gather from James 1:6 and Hebrews 6:19 below.

_____
_____

You have studied hard today but before we close there is one more gem you're not going to want to miss! Please turn and savor Acts 11:1-18. _____

Peter was a man of God as we can see this event started while Peter was in prayer (vs. 5). God gives Peter a message with a mission and at first like Joseph it goes against everything he knows. Verse 8 (NLT) begins with Peter responding to the Lord, *"'No, Lord,'* Peter thinks he knows better. Does this sound familiar?

Peter was a man who was walking closely with God and yet he was hit with the unexpected, the inconvenient, and that which the rest of the world did not understand. But in the end like Joseph, Mary and the shepherds, Peter chooses to humble himself under God's mighty hand (1 Peter 5:6) and acknowledge that His ways are so much higher than mere human ways (Isaiah 55:8-9)!

Here is one to tuck in your heart's pocket:
Acts 11:17 (NLT) *And since God… who am I to stand in God's way?"*

Peter chose to trust and found God faithful. He became an instrumental part in the turning of the early church to include the Gentiles, all people! Who can stand against the power and movement of the Holy Spirit!
Will we get out of our own way? Will we get out of God's way and choose instead to be used in His way? For the best way?

As we close today please spend a moment in prayer asking God to help you formulate your response to all He has spoken to your heart today.

_____
_____
_____
_____

Day 6 & 7: At His Feet – A Time to Reflect

Over the next two days take time to reflect over your week of study. Maybe you need some time to catch up on the study material and this might be the perfect break to do just that with the Lord!

I encourage you to glance back at the final point at the end of each day that you recorded having had the greatest impact on your heart. As you spend time with God in prayer, reflect and record on the lines below how God is tying it together and applying it to your life specifically for such a time as this.

Ask that God make it clear who He would have you invite into a natural opportunity to share Him, to apply what you are learning; maybe a child, grandchild, friend... trust Him to continue to take the lead. May we have a heart ever ready with eyes and ears out to the opportunities God wants to invite us into for His glory and praise.

Do not merely listen to the word, and so deceive yourselves. Do what it says. Anyone who listens to the word but does not do what it says is like someone who looks at his face in a mirror and, after looking at himself, goes away and immediately forgets what he looks like. But whoever looks intently into the perfect law that gives freedom, and continues in it – not forgetting what they have heard, but doing it – they will be blessed in what they do. James 1:22-25 (NIV)

_____

_____

_____

_____

_____

_____

_____

_____

Philippians 4:13 (NIV) *I can do all this through him who gives me strength.*

John 14:26 (NIV) *But the Advocate, the Holy Spirit, whom the Father will send in my name, will teach you all things and will remind you of everything I have said to you.*

WEEK 3

But when you ask him, be sure that your faith is in God alone. Do not waver, for a person with divided loyalty is as unsettled as a wave of the sea that is blown and tossed by the wind. James 1:6 (NLT)

Day 1: A Good Father

Hi, dearly beloved child of God. Welcome back!! Let us pray that we receive the presence of the Lord with open hearts and minds as we begin our study today of His Word. *Satisfy us in the morning with your unfailing love, that we may sing for joy and be glad all our days.* Psalm 90:14 (NIV)

A verse to tuck in our hearts: *He said, "I came naked from my mother's womb, and I will be naked when I leave. The LORD gave me what I had, and the LORD has taken it away. Praise the name of the LORD!"* Job 1:21 (NLT)

Praise the name of the Lord! Romans 11:35 (NIV) states, *"Who has ever given to God, that God should repay them?"* How easily do we fall into the pit of thinking God owes us?! God Almighty sacrificed His one and only Son that whosoever would believe in Him would have eternal life (John 3:16)! What else are we thinking we deserve? If we get nothing else, we have our salvation from all the brokenness of this world!!!

Psalm 103:1-5 reminds us of the benefits of the Lord. Please record below the list of things described in these verses.

_____

_____

_____

_____

_____

Ephesians 4:8 (NKJV) tells us, *Therefore He says: "When He ascended on high, He led captivity captive, And gave gifts to men."*

Jesus conquered the grave and led CAPTIVITY CAPTIVE!!! Does that not resonate with anyone else out there like it does me?!! Hallelujah and Amen!

Take a moment and savor Job 38. _____

How is THAT for some perspective!! Yet read Psalm 8 and tell me that does not put you in the love seat of awestruck humility with me?!

How good and great is our God!!

Today let us continue where we left off in Scripture yesterday. Please read Luke 2:21-32. _____

Luke 2:21 indicates that just like we studied about John the Baptist, Jesus was also given His name spoken over Him even before His birth. Matthew 1:21 (NLT) *And she will have a son, and you are to name him Jesus, for he will save his people from their sins."*

Acts 4:11-12 (NIV) *Jesus is "'the stone you builders rejected, which has become the cornerstone.' Salvation is found in no one else, for there is no other name under heaven given to mankind by which we must be saved."*

Please fill in the blanks below according to John 14:6 (NIV).

Jesus answered, "I am the _____ and the _____ and the _____. No one comes to the Father except through me.
(Way, Truth, Life)

That is not limiting but rather liberating isn't it?!! He has made the way simple, no questions or guessing and making wrong turns and getting lost. Just one Way - JESUS! Jesus is the Way! He is Savior God, the Way to eternal life!

We read in Luke 2:21-24 Mary and Joseph were presenting their son to God. Jewish families went through different ceremonies after a child was born. A boy was circumcised and named on the eighth day. One month after birth a first-born son was to be presented to God and through an offering was considered redeemed or bought back. (See Exodus 13:2, 11-16 and Num.18:15-16) The parents were acknowledging to Who this life they were entrusted to steward for such a time as this, truly belonged to. In addition, after a birth the mother was considered unclean and after a certain number of days the parents were to bring a lamb for a burnt offering and a dove or a pigeon as a sin offering. If the lamb were too expensive the family could bring a second bird as Mary and Joseph did.

What were Jewish parents acknowledging through these ceremonies that we too must acknowledge if we are to truly steward our gifts from Him well?

_____

That their child really belonged to God, only God can give life, so really that child is only on loan to us as guardians to help raise them to know their Creator God. He has a GREAT purpose for each life He breathes His breath into!! As parents or guardians of a young life let us pray to hold on loosely as we fiercely love them to Jesus.

Hold loosely, love fiercely.

We also learn from this passage that they were not wealthy by the world's standards But yet in God's eyes they were just rollin' rich in the kind of love He desired to be lavished on His one and only Son! I do not think you can get any wealthier than that! How wealthy are you in the thing's money cannot buy? List those things you have that cannot be bought below.

_____

_____

_____

When you have something that precious you know you are really rollin' rich! Praise Him!!

"A person cannot receive even one thing unless it is given him from heaven. (John 3:27 ESV) Considering what you just wrote down in regards to what you possess that no amount of money could have earned you, in light of John 3:27 (above), what insight does this give you into His lavish love for you?

_____

_____

Read Matthew 7:11.

Our God is a good, good Father and longs to be gracious to you (Isaiah 30:18)!

As we close please spend time thanking Him for His blessings in your life and then record below that which made the most impact on your heart today.

_____

_____

_____

_____

Day 2: No Other Name

Hi there! I am so extremely glad you have been so dedicated in your study. I know life can have many demands, distractions and pressures for our time. God of the universe has not missed the ways you have chosen to place Him first. Please begin in prayer. I am praising Him that our God who keeps the world spinning on its axis is still never too busy to spend time with us!

Continuing from yesterday please glance back over Luke 2:21-32 and then fill in the blank below.

Luke 2:25-32 describes a man named _____.

Simeon was righteous and devout and EAGERLY WAITING my NLT tells me in Luke 2:25! Do you feel you have been waiting on God for something so long your eagerness has been lost?

_____

I wonder if Simeon ever wrestled with doubt. Maybe every year he got a little bit older and still he waited…

The beginning of Luke 2:28 (NLT) affirms for me that even if he did waver now and again, he never gave in because *Simeon was there*. He was in the right place at the right time because he held onto the promise God had given him, he held onto the hope that does not disappoint and He was able to hold that promise in his arms!

Unlike the world's hope, God's hope is sure! Romans 5:5 (NKJV) *Now hope does not disappoint, because the love of God has been poured out in our hearts by the Holy Spirit who was given to us.* 2 Corinthians 1:21-22 (NIV) *Now it is God who makes both us and you stand firm in Christ. He anointed us, set his seal of ownership on us, and put his Spirit in our hearts as a deposit, guaranteeing what is to come.*

Luke 2:26 states that Simeon had received the promise that he would not die until he had seen "the Lord's Messiah (or the Lord's Anointed)".[v]
What does Isaiah 61:1-3 tell us He was anointed to do?

_____
_____
_____
_____

Again, how good and great is our God!

(Luke 2:32 NLT) *He is a light to reveal God to the nations,*

Now that Jesus has ascended to heaven… until His return what are we called to be? See Matthew 5:13-16.

———————————————————————

———————————————————————

Salt and Light! Salt is a preservative. How are you preserving the Good News for this and the next generation? How are you carrying the Light of Truth around inside you for all to see in thought, word and action throughout your circle of influence? *That circle starts close to home. The last part of Matthew 5:15 (NLT) states, *a lamp is placed on a stand, where it gives light to everyone in the house.* Ministry starts with the family.

———————————————————————

———————————————————————

We must stand for something or we will fall for anything - a non-decision is a decision. What warning does Revelation 3:16 and Matthew 10:33 give us?

———————————————————————

———————————————————————

John 12:43 (NLT) *For they loved human praise more than praise from God.*

Dear one, let's stand with the One who's name is Faithful and True (Rev. 19:11), who knows all our sin (past, present and future) and yet chose to stand in our place and give Himself for us… anyway!

- One day the choice will be gone… God Almighty will be honored by all.

It is written: "'As surely as I live,' says the Lord, 'every knee will bow before me; every tongue will acknowledge God.'" Romans 14:11 (NIV)
- Jesus is God our Savior.

- The richest people are those with treasures money cannot buy - the gift of eternal life is free because Jesus paid it all.

- Do not give up hope on God's faithful promises spoken in His Word.

The grass withers and the flowers fall, but the word of our God endures forever." Isaiah 40:8 (NIV)

Thank you sincerely for today dear one. Now go be salt and light for our God!

God bless you muchly~

Please take a moment to record what stood out to you the most from today's study.

_____

_____

_____

_____

Day 3: Eagerly Waiting

Hello dearly beloved of God. I am sure you have experienced "eagerly waiting". Probably safe to say you have eagerly waited more times than you have been eager to wait, am I right!?! I do not know that I have ever been eager to wait in my life! Well… I take that back I would not mind pushing off a visit to the dentist! Even though I do have the sweetest dentist it is just not the place I am eager to go to. What about you? Is there anything you are eagerly waiting on now?

_____

May we trust that if it is on our mind, it is on His heart dear one.

Before we go too much further let us bow and ask that God Almighty breathe His breath into us that will bring intelligence for receiving His Word way beyond our own capacity! (Job 32:8)

To tuck in your heart's pocket: Philippians 3:8 (ESV) *Indeed, I count everything as loss because of the surpassing worth of knowing Christ Jesus my Lord. For his sake I have suffered the loss of all things and count them as rubbish, in order that I may gain Christ*

What advice does Luke 14:28-30 give us?

_____

_____

45

Count the cost of being His disciple.

These verses might help with the "count". After you explore each one (or pick one or two for now and just highlight the rest as treasures to circle back to at another time) respond with what God lays on your heart toward Him after your readings. Philippians 1:6 ___, Matthew 6:19-21, 24 ___, Matthew 24:13 ___, John 16:33 ___, John 12:25 ___, John 14:2-3 ___, 1 Corinthians 2:9 ___, 2 Corinthians 4:17 ___, Revelation 21:3-4 ___

_____

_____

_____

_____

This world is broken, and broken things happen to any human but in Christ we have a guarantee that we do not ultimately end broken! Oh, praise Him! Please read Romans 8:31-39. _____

John 10:28 (NIV) *I give them eternal life, and they shall never perish; no one will snatch them out of my hand.*

Life in this world can be hard (especially in the waiting room) but the One whose grip on your life will not fail has overcome this world - let Him hang on to you dear one!!

Please read Luke 2:33-38. _____

In Luke 2:33-35 we see Simeon speak a prophecy concerning the life of Jesus. With Jesus there would be no neutral ground. Remember lukewarm gets spit out (Rev. 3:16)! A choice must be made, the God of the universe who gave Himself up for us not only deserves a decision but requires one! You cannot kind of believe He is God and sort of not. He either is or is not to you and that determines the course of your entire life eternally!

Some would stumble over this Truth and some would receive it. What is the difference between Isaiah 8:14-15 and Malachi 4:2?

_____

_____

Let's remind ourselves what Matthew 11:6 (NKJV) tells us, *And blessed is he who is not offended because of Me."*

Let us not lose salvation because we cannot in our finite mind understand all the details, all the why's, how's and when's! In any real relationship true love cannot be forced and it involves a trust and a faith in the other person. God has given us His faithful Word and proven trustworthy time and time again all throughout Scripture! He is the same yesterday, today and forever (Heb. 13:8) we can trust Him with all our unknowns.

John 12:7 (NLT) *Jesus replied, "You don't understand now what I am doing, but someday you will."*
What does Luke 2:35 tell us will happen to Mary?

_____

Maybe some of you feel like you can relate on some level with having your soul pierced. Mary would experience great pain at seeing her... or rather God's Son rejected and crucified. As Jesus is God's Son not Mary's so are the loved ones in yours and my life. As much as we want to cling to them as ours, they are in fact God's. As hard as it is to imagine He loves them more and has a greater purpose for their life than we can fathom. A bird held, cannot fly. We pray to be able to hold those He has entrusted to us for such a time as this up to Him with open hands so they can fly with the wings He gave them.

Please write 2 Timothy 1:12 below.

_____

_____

_____

Have we entrusted our loved ones to Him? Then we can know, we can be convinced that He is able to guard that which we have entrusted to Him!!!! Oh, my dear friend I am so stuffing this one into my hearts pocket for sure!

Between Luke 2:36 and verse 38 who enters our saga?

_____

Anna. Like Simeon, she was a devoted worshiper of God Almighty. She too was in the right place at the right time! I think this no coincidence but rather showing us that when we walk with God, He only leads us to the right place at the right time! Sometimes like Mary and Joseph arriving at the stable at first what seems doomed may turn out to be divine! Verse 38 in my NLT tells me, *She talked about the child to everyone who had been waiting expectantly for God*

The ones who were waiting expectantly like Simeon, "eagerly waiting", those were the ones who received the blessing. Remember what it says in Isaiah 30:18 (NIV)? *Blessed are all who wait for him!*

Do we live our days in eager expectation for His return? Matthew 24:36 (NKJV) *But of that day and hour no one knows, not even the angels of heaven, but My Father only.*

2 Timothy 4:2 (NLT) gives us all good advice since none of us know just when He will come back! *Be prepared, whether the time is favorable or not.*

Today has been quite a trek through Scripture dear one! Thanks for sticking with it! I hope you felt it was well worth the cost of your time and effort as much as I did! I am already eagerly awaiting your presence back here tomorrow! Before you go please take a moment to record what God used to impact your heart the most within our study today.

_____

_____

_____

_____

Day 4: Cost Count (part 1)

Hello my friend! A genuine friendship is one of those things that cannot be bought, it is priceless. However, on the other hand genuine friendship does cost. It is written in marriage vows… "in sickness and in health" meaning at the cost of my own agenda I will stick by you even when it inconveniences me, when it costs me something.

When two people decide to take the next step into marriage, to commit to each other "until death do us part" they seemingly have "counted the cost" of what that will mean. Much of what that means is unknown! It is a choice up front without knowing all the details to choose "us" over "me" at every fork in the road life may bring, why… because of love.

I am praying that it may be purely His love that compels us today in all things. 2 Corinthians 5:14 (NIV) begins, *For Christ's love compels us,* by His amazing grace it is not our love for Him but rather His great for us that is the driving force behind our very lives.

Meet you on the other side of Matthew 2:1-18. _____

Most nativity scenes today depict there being three wise men, but the Scripture mentions three gifts, it could have been a whole group of wise men! It is likely Jesus was one or two years old by the time the wise men found Him. It is also interesting to note that gold was for royalty, frankincense for deity, and myrrh a spice used to prepare a body for burial.

I do not know if the wisemen knew the full impact their gifts had in foreshadowing the Truth about just who this baby Jesus was! Such a reminder that when we bring our best to God He is able to do far beyond what we ever could have imagined with it! Are you willing to offer your absolute best to God without excuse? Take a moment to contemplate what is on your heart to offer Him and then if need be ask Him to help you trust Him more in order to lay aside any excuses that have held you back. Record your thoughts below.

_____

_____

We see the wise men pose a question in verse 2 that is remarkably like King Herod's in verse 4. What is the question everyone wants answers to?

_____

Where...? Have you ever had a "where?" question for God? What did you do about it? Did you feel like you received an answer or direction from God? How did you know it was Him guiding you?

_____

_____

_____

What does King Herod do to get his question answered?

_____

He calls together wise counsel, *the leading priests and teachers of religious law* (Matthew 2:4 NLT).

What is the counsel of these men (verses 5-6)?

_____

_____

They quote Scripture! Look up Micah 5:2 and compare it with Matthew 2:6!

Psalm 119:105 (NIV) *Your word is a lamp for my feet, a light on my path.*

What lit the wise man's path (Matthew 2:9)?

_____

The star went AHEAD of them and led them directly WHERE they needed to be one step at a time. The wise men kept their gaze upward until they reached their destination.

Psalm 139:5 tells us what?

_____

_____

2 Timothy 4:18 re-assures us of what?

_____

_____

Hebrews 12:2 reminds us to fix our gaze where?

_____

_____

Fix our gaze on Whom our victory rests and trust He can make an arrival for us in His Kingdom unharmed as He promises to be our protection on all sides. Again, this in no way means this side of heaven will be easy for us or for any human being for that matter. We will have "where?" questions but if we are WHERE He is, we are WHERE we are supposed to be! Like Simeon; like Anna; when we are walking in authentic relationship with our God will always be at the right place at the right time. Remember that may look different than you expected just like it probably did for Mary as she rolled up to give birth in a barn! However, as Psalm 84:10 (NIV) reminds us, *Better is one day in your courts than thousands elsewhere; I would rather be a doorkeeper in the house of my God than dwell in the tents of the wicked.*

Stay in His guiding light. Psalm 36:9 (NIV) *For with you is the fountain of life; in your light we see light.*

In Matthew 2:13-18 we see once again the willingness of Joseph to follow obediently the command of his God without hesitation and without question.

Notice yet again the events occurring here have been previously prophesied! We see the Old Testament foreshadowing the life of Jesus in the New Testament! As a young nation Israel was let to Egypt during a famine (see Gen. 46:1-4) just as Jesus was led there as a child. And just as Israel was protected and brought out so was Jesus. Hosea 11:1 (NIV) *"When Israel was child, I loved him, and out of Egypt I called my son.* The Old Testament points forward to Jesus Christ and this is another example of God's Sovereignty and faithfulness through all generations.

Our passage in Matthew tells us God awoke Joseph in a dream and that very night Joseph responded. When God calls us out, how quickly, how readily do we respond? It could be calling us out of our comfort zone to serve or forgive or show grace and mercy... We could phrase this question another way... how willing are we to stay put, remain still, wait when that is His call on our lives for a time? Respond to the question below that most resonates with you in this current season of your life.

_____

_____

Judges 15:18-19 records a time when Sampson was extremely thirsty to the point he feared death after a battle (A battle where he killed 1,000 men with a single jawbone of a donkey - wild I know, we would be thirsty too!!) Sampson cries out to God and God answers by causing water to gush out of a hollow in the ground! Sampson calls the place "The Spring of the One Who Cried Out". That is beautiful!

What does John 7:37-39 declare?

_____

_____

Hebrews 11:6 (NLT) states, *And it is impossible to please God without faith. Anyone who wants to come to him must believe that God exists and that he rewards those who sincerely seek him.*

Anyone who comes, anyone who cries out to Him must believe and in believing you will receive His Living Water the gift of the Holy Spirit and eternal life.

John 14:26 (ESV) *But the Helper, the Holy Spirit, whom the Father will send in my name, he will teach you all things and bring to your remembrance all that I have said to you.*

So when we find ourselves in the middle of what feels like great cost as we faithfully walk out our obedience to the one who paid the ultimate cost for our life remember as a believer you have the Holy Spirit, He is God with us, you are not alone.

The waiting room of life is difficult, yet the Author of time does not waste it dear one. He has great purpose even in the waiting room.

Carrying your cross for Christ is costly however Christ took ours all the way to hell, so our journey only ends in victory! Keep going, in Christ you were made to carry His victory!

Please record how God impacted your heart the most today and thank you ever so very muchly for studying today dear one.

_____
_____
_____
_____

Day 5: Cost Count (part 2)

Hello friend. I pray today's study in His Word will stir such a fire for passionate perseverance in Him that it will be uncontainable! So uncontainable that its spark will be contagious, lighting up everyone in our sphere of influence to His glory and praise!

Please begin in prayer in order to prepare the soil of our hearts to receive the seed of His Word.

As we begin a bit off the beat path, please sit back and savor chapters 6 and 7 of the book of Acts. _____

How does Acts 6:5 and verse 8 describe Stephen?

_____

I gather from those verses that being full of faith, grace and the Holy Spirit equals power! Stephen was a man ready in season and out of season because when the need arose for seven good men (verse 3) Stephen's name came to mind.

According to verse two he was chosen to "serve tables" (ESV)! From Stephen's speech in Acts 7 he was clearly overqualified for the position and yet he stepped up willingly. If we are not willing to be on the top of our game out of season, we won't be on the top of our game in season.

Acts 6:11 tells us Stephen was falsely accused yet his countenance remains one of what? (See verse 15.)

_____

Stephan was under the strength and power of the Holy Spirit. What else does the Holy Spirit help us with according to Matthew 10:19?

_____

_____

We see proof of this Truth all throughout Acts chapter 7!! What many would see as a problem, Stephen saw as an opportunity to further the Kingdom! How much is the Kingdom cause at the top of our thoughts and the motivator of our words and actions?

_____

_____

Stephen's speech throws everyone into a rage (Acts 7:54) but Stephen remains steady, his gaze fixed toward heaven just like the wisemen's. What did Stephen see as he was about to be murdered? (See Acts 7:55.)

Jesus standing. Jesus stood for us on the cross and stands for us now. Romans 8:34 (NIV) *Who then is the one who condemns? No one. Christ Jesus who died--more than that, who was raised to life--is at the right hand of God and is also interceding for us.*

Stephen was considered one of the seven good men! We might want to desperately cry out, "why God, why Stephen?!"

Stephen was taken to paradise that day and I doubt he was wanting to come back here! "Remember Stephen's death had a profound impact on Paul, who later became the world's greatest missionary."[vi] The very same Paul who was first named Saul and in Acts 8:1 is said to have been a witness to the whole murdering event, agreeing completely with Stephens killing!

Saul turned Paul is one of the greatest reversals of all time! Saul/Paul changed the WORLD and still is today with the way God used him to write His Word down in quite a chunk of the New Testament for us!

Stephen was a man sold out for God Almighty. He had counted the cost. Remember the verse we first tucked in our pocket on day 3 of this week?

Philippians 3:8 (ESV) *Indeed, I count everything as loss because of the surpassing worth of knowing Christ Jesus my Lord. For his sake I have suffered the loss of all things and count them as rubbish, in order that I may gain Christ* … Stephen had counted the cost and declared it worth his very life.

You know… Philippians was written by none other than Saul/Paul himself. If it had not been for Stephen who had first counted the cost and thought it well worth paying maybe Paul never would have seen the Light and then what?! Each life that stands for Christ, that counts the cost and finds it a privilege to suffer for the One who suffered to offer them/us the free gift of eternity is a world changer, a Kingdom changer, upping the population of Heaven while depleting that of hell!

So, when we cry out, "why Stephen God?!" The answer is because Stephen was willing to let his life count for something bigger than himself. What cost his life, brought the Word to us. Will we allow God to use us for a higher purpose - to expand His Kingdom, to bring the Word to another? We must all count the cost and decide if it is worth it. Stephen did, Paul did, Jesus did... and we were saved.

Will we allow God to use our life for all that He dreamed of when He first thought of us?! May we all...count everything as loss because of the surpassing worth of knowing Christ Jesus...

Thank you muchly for sticking with your study of His Word~

Please spend time in prayer as you decide what God impacted your heart with the most from today's study.

_____

_____

_____

_____

Day 6 & 7: At His Feet – A Time to Reflect

Over the next two days take time to reflect over your week of study. Maybe you need some time to catch up on the study material and this might be the perfect break to do just that with the Lord!

I encourage you to glance back at the final point at the end of each day that you recorded having had the greatest impact on your heart. As you spend time with God in prayer, reflect and record on the lines below how God is tying it together and applying it to your life specifically for such a time as this.

Ask that God make it clear who He would have you invite into an opportunity to share Him, to apply what you are learning; maybe a child, grandchild, friend... trust Him to continue to take the lead. May we have a heart ever ready with eyes and ears out to the opportunities God wants to invite us into for His glory and praise.

Do not merely listen to the word, and so deceive yourselves. Do what it says. Anyone who listens to the word but does not do what it says is like someone who looks at his face in a mirror and, after looking at himself, goes away and immediately forgets what he looks like.

But whoever looks intently into the perfect law that gives freedom, and continues in it – not forgetting what they have heard, but doing it – they will be blessed in what they do. James 1:22-25 (NIV)

_____

_____

_____

_____

_____

_____

_____

_____

_____

Philippians 4:13 (NIV) *I can do all this through him who gives me strength.*

John 14:26 (NIV) *But the Advocate, the Holy Spirit, whom the Father will send in my name, will teach you all things and will remind you of everything I have said to you.*

WEEK 4

Then Christ will make his home in your hearts as you trust in him. Your roots will grow down into God's love and keep you strong. Ephesians 3:17 (NLT)

Day 1: Let It Grow

Thank you for sticking with me thus far! Let's bow as we praise God for this time together and ask that He lead us deeper into the good soil of His heart knowing it's only God that makes the seed grow. (1 Corinthians 3:7)

Before we begin, go ahead and tuck this in your hearts pocket today: *So let it grow, for when your endurance is fully developed, you will be perfect and complete, needing nothing.* James 1:4 (NLT)

The verse just before that pocket verse is James 1:3 (obviously) and it tells us, (NLT) *For you know that when your faith is tested, your endurance has a chance to grow.*

The testing of our faith… hmmm I don't know about you but I loathed tests in school, so when it comes to spiritual tests I don't imagine I'd call myself a much bigger fan of those either! BUT when faith is tested our endurance has a chance to grow... and who does not want greater endurance?!! As a cross country runner (in the past... distant past) I can attest to the extreme value of a high level of endurance! (Honestly, anyone caring for young children can attest to the extreme value of high levels of endurance, am I right!?!) So that is why James 1:4, our pocket verse starts out with... LET - IT - GROW!!

Do not give up in the testing. As in a running race, fix your eyes on your next goal and keep running, you will make it. Once you make it to the water station (because obviously that must be everyone's goal, right?! Just make it to the next water station!) you fill up and fix your eyes on the next goal (the next water station or maybe by now the finish line - in Jesus we all have Heaven as our finish line or rather more like our starting line!).

God's Word, His Holy Spirit is our Living Water that never runs out. We will have enough to fuel our hearts as we keep on through the testing, allowing our endurance to grow, strengthening us to not only cross the finish line but to cross it in a full on spiritual sprint; for His glory.

One of my favorite quotes by Erma Bombeck is, "When I stand before God at the end of my life, I would hope that I would not have a single bit of talent left, and could say, 'I used everything you gave me'."

Please read Matthew 2:19-23. _____

Verse 19 begins with, (NLT) *When Herod died*, what happens immediately following that event as indicated in the rest of verse 19 and into 20?

_____

This shows me that our God is a God who sees (Gen. 16:13) AND engages to work out His purpose on earth as it is in heaven (Matthew 6:10).

"Am I only a God nearby," declares the LORD, "and not a God far away? Who can hide in secret places so that I cannot see them?" declares the LORD. "Do not I fill heaven and earth?" declares the LORD. Jeremiah 23:23-24 (NIV)

On Joseph's way back to Israel what emotion caused a hesitation (Matt. 2:22)?

_____

However, in Joseph's fear God supplied what (again in verse 22)?

_____

Direction. In Joseph's uneasiness God provided His wisdom and direction of which Joseph listened to and followed.

If we feel a hesitation in our hearts or minds about something let us allow God time to offer clarification through His Word and in prayer. Maybe it is nothing and He will embolden our confidence to proceed forward or maybe He will give guidance to alter our approach and or direction. He is faithful and desires that we walk in His way so He will not hide it if we are willing to trust and walk in His leading footsteps.

We can pray for God to heighten our awareness of things that are not right. As a parent or guardian or even as a friend we can pray for God to give us that sixth sense to realize when something is not quite right with any of our children not to condemn but rather to restore them to the way that leads to everlasting life in a way that is filled with His wisdom and love.

Alright, meet you over in Luke 2:39-52. _____

In Luke 2:40 we see a description of Jesus that is remarkably like a description of John the Baptist in Luke 1:80. Please compare these two verses below in your own words.

_____

_____

These are definitely verses to turn into prayers over all the young in our life! (And maybe even the not so young… if we are breathing this side of heaven, we are ALL still a work in progress. Let us pray we grow in wisdom, stature and favor with God and people (Luke 2:52).)

Luke 2:40 creates a frame of sorts with Luke 2:52. Take a moment to compare both bookend verses. These verses frame for me an astounding picture of Jesus' wisdom (even at 12 years old).

In this picture frame of sorts, we see Mary and Joseph lose something… what is it or should I say WHO is it?! _____

We have all had our moments of parenting disasters but losing God kind of tops the list does it not!?!! It happens to be Mother's Day here and can I say I am just so incredibly grateful God has given my six children hearts so full of His grace.

Where was Jesus found (verse 46)?

_____

Jesus was not panicked like His earthly parents were. Psalm 139 makes it quite clear that God cannot lose you. Even if we feel we have lost Him He has not lost us. Feeling lost?! Go worship Him in His sanctuary, pray at the foot of the cross and you are sure to find Him there every time dear one.

Please write out the question found in Luke 2:48 below.

_____

It is a "why?" question. Have you ever had a similar question for God? (NLT) *"why have you done this to us?*

_____
_____
_____

Jesus' answer in verse 49 points us all to His higher purpose. He had come to earth not to be their son but to fulfill the will of the Father. Maybe the answer to our "Why…?" is because of a higher purpose that we do not yet quite fully understand.

Luke 2:50 relays to us that Jesus' parents did not understand His answer at that time yet according to verse 51 what does Mary do?

_____

She treasures it all in her heart.

We all, like Mary, have a choice to make in all that we do not understand about the way our God works. We can become offended and walk away, becoming bitter and hardened. Or we can tuck it into our heart as a moment to discuss with our Heavenly Father when we see Him face to face one day. For now, we can choose to trust that He is good, and works all things together for good (Romans 8:28). We can choose to allow our "Why's…?" to become faith fertilizer.

So, let it grow.

All who heard him were amazed at his understanding and his answers. Luke 2:47 (NLT) One day, if we do not give up but stand firm on His faithful, enduring Word, we will be amazed at His understanding in our misunderstanding and His answers in all our questions. Receiving His peace within the questions makes needing the answers less urgent.

Mary chose to let it go, in a sense that she would not let what she did not know trip her up from the God she did. Mary chose instead to tuck it into her heart so that in His time, the One she knew, could grow it into a beautiful understanding of His higher purpose.

This has become such a treasured time of traveling together in His Word. Thank you for joining me.

Please finish out today in prayer, recording that which touched your heart the most.

_____

_____

_____

_____

Day 2: Greater Than I

Welcome beloved of God, I am so extremely glad to have you back! I have been praying for you. I am praying that God, who declares His Word to be like fire (Jer. 23:29) will use it as a refiner's fire to purify our hearts' love for Him. That we might love Him with wholehearted devotion and desire to serve Him with an undivided loyalty. Before we officially step into this week of study let us individually step into His lap thanking Him for this opportunity to study His Word and that as He leads, He graciously helps us follow.

Today we will begin our comparison of four different segments of Scripture.

Matthew 3:1-12, Mark 1:1-8, Luke 3:1-18 and John 1:19-28. We will only be looking at the segment in John for now, the other three perspectives we will dive into later this week.

Please begin by reading the segment in John 1:19-28. _____

Imagine being in a job interview. How many of us, if we were asked, "Who are you?" would start off with what we are NOT?! Maybe we know we are not the BEST at something but typically that is not what we want to highlight right off. Yet that is what we see John the Baptist do in verse 20! The Pharisees had seen the great following of John and probably not just a little jealous, wanted to see what he was all about.

In a situation like this John had every opportunity to take advantage and promote his fame, however we see in sobering humility, John answers the Pharisees first question with direct and to the point clarity, *"I am not the Messiah."* John 1:20 (NLT). He left no room for debate or contemplation, no grey area, he was NOT the Messiah, period.

I wonder if we do not consciously think we are the Messiah but subconsciously our actions display a different stance.

Please read James 3:13-18 and record the contrast between worldly wisdom and godly wisdom within the chart on the following page.

Worldly Wisdom:	Godly Wisdom:

A good way to self-check what kind of wisdom we are using in our decision making is to first pray Psalm 139:24 (NLT), *Point out anything in me that offends you, and lead me along the path of everlasting life.*

What we think or the way we think governs our actions, so it is especially important what wisdom we receive our motivation from.

Following the checklist of godly wisdom attributes in your box above, be honest in self evaluating any actions you may be participating in or thinking of participating in. Is your motive pure (really), is it peace loving (really), is it always gentle, is it willing to yield to others (really), is it full (yes full) of mercy, good deeds, does it show favoritism, is it truly sincere (really)...?! If on any of these accounts we feel shady then we should go back and ask God for more of that refiner's fire so that when He tests us we will come out as pure as gold (Job 23:10).

As the conversation in John continues between John the Baptist and the Pharisees, we can see he had multiple chances to make himself into more than he was but at each turn he remained humble.

In John 1:26 (NLT) John tells them, *"I baptize with water, but right here in the crowd is someone you do not recognize.*

"Right here in the crowd…" Jesus is Immanuel and right there in the crowds with us! Joshua 1:9 (NIV) states, *Have I not commanded you? Be strong and courageous. Do not be afraid; do not be discouraged, for the LORD your God will be with you wherever you go."*

You do not stand alone in a crowd, not ever. Is there any situation or circumstance that in tucking this Truthful promise found in Joshua 1:9 into your hearts pocket, would be most beneficial to you?

_____

John 1:26 (NLT) finishes with, *"...someone you do not recognize."* reminds me of Hebrews 13:2 (NIV) *Do not forget to show hospitality to strangers, for by so doing some people have shown hospitality to angels without knowing it.* There is always someone watching that we may not recognize or realize is watching us. What are they perceiving, learning or picking up from us? May we always be people of integrity inside and out.

When John could not verify himself as someone the Pharisees thought was professionally important what or who does John quote in John 1:23?

_____

God's Word through the prophet Isaiah!

John allowed God's Word to matter more to him, to hold more weight in his heart, to guide his purpose, to validate his worth, to sustain and guide him more than what people said about him. John turns their attention to Scripture, Isaiah 40:3.

Isaiah also states in 55:11 (NIV), *so is my word that goes out from my mouth: It will not return to me empty, but will accomplish what I desire and achieve the purpose for which I sent it.* When you feel ineffective, know His Word never is, it is ALWAYS effective and accomplishes His purpose.

What do the Pharisees ask John next in John 1:25?

_____

They assume he is just an unqualified "nobody". They ask him what right he has to baptize?!

This reminds me of Amos. Please look up Amos 7:12-15.
We see Amos, like John, receive less than a warm welcome. John was just John and Amos was just Amos. Amos 7:14-15 (NLT) *But Amos replied, "I'm not a professional prophet, and I was never trained to be one. I'm just a shepherd, and I take care of sycamore-fig trees. But the Lord called me away from my flock and told me, 'Go and prophesy to my people in Israel.'*

In all that Amos may have felt unqualified for he answered the call of God faithfully trusting that if God called him, He would adequately qualify him for the job. He did not shrink back in fear or succumb to the comfort zone of the fig trees. Amos stepped out with God as untrained and unprofessional as he felt and trusted the professionalism of God, that the Almighty knew what He was doing when He called him.

How willing do you think you are to step out with God? I pray to be more willing but also need to pray to be willing to be more willing if that makes sense?! It goes with counting the cost and praying that He always has the first seat in my life no matter what, or if, or even when, the call is something I feel quite unqualified for.

Could you fill in those verses (recorded in full above) from Amos according to your own life?

...I'm not a professional _____, I was never trained to be _____. I'm just a _____, and I take care of _____. But the Lord called me...

What was it that made a calling on your life clear to you that it was from God?
_____
_____

Maybe you feel unclear as to what God has called you to. I think sometimes we overcomplicate it. (Sometimes I overcomplicate it!) Could it be as simple as seeing a need that is right in front of you that you have the ability or resource to meet and just stepping forward to meet it? Our spiritual gifting is God's way of loving others through us. He has called us all to be faithful right where He has us. Loving people in our sphere of influence well, anyways and always.

A dear friend of mine has a sweatshirt that if it were mine, would be one of my favorites. It is this big grey comfy looking sweatshirt with the words across the front in big bold lettering, "LOVE ANYWAYS".

What are the greatest two commandments in the law? (See Matthew 22:36-40)
_____
_____

Love.

What does Matthew 7:2, 5 tell us happens when we choose to slide our caboose in God's Judgment seat?
_____
_____

Careful, that seat is a hot one!!

What example does Jesus give us in Romans 5:8 for demonstrating His love?

_____

He loved us anyway! He saved our cabooses ANYWAY! So then what right do we have for not giving out of the love He has so lavished on us (Romans 5:5)?!!

We are all called to the extraordinary… to LOVE ANYWAY. If we never hear another word from God on our calling, we all have enough to keep us busy in "LOVING ANYWAY" for the rest of our lives, wouldn't y'all agree!?!!

So back to John the Baptist and the question regarding his ability to baptize. John was baptizing Jews which normally were only baptized for purification reasons. Usually Gentiles were baptized when they converted to Judaism. The Pharisees were wondering why John was treating the chosen Jewish people like Gentiles. John was baptizing with water, only helping the people with a symbolic act of repentance. Soon Jesus would come, the only One who could truly forgive sin. (*Life Application Study Bible* notes, 1976)

In John 1:27 John the Baptist makes it clear he sees himself not even worthy to be called Jesus' slave. Though this is true of all of us how has God chosen to treat us?

Galatians 3:26 (NLT) states, *For you are all children of God through faith in Christ Jesus.* Wow!

We would all do well to have the reverential holy fear that John had in his heart toward God. Please read the following Scriptures and write out your heart's response below. 1 Peter 5:6, Proverbs 9:10, 1 Corinthians 1:27, Psalm 8:3-4.

_____
_____
_____

John the Baptist's life consistently pointed to the One he knew to be greater than him. May it be said of us. Thank you for a great study dear one! Please take a moment to record how God impacted your heart today.

_____

_____

_____

_____

Day 3: Inexpressible Joy

So be truly glad. There is wonderful joy ahead, even though you have to endure many trials for a little while. These trials will show that your faith is genuine. It is being tested as fire tests and purifies gold—though your faith is far more precious than mere gold. So when your faith remains strong through many trials, it will bring you much praise and glory and honor on the day when Jesus Christ is revealed to the whole world. You love him even though you have never seen him. Though you do not see him now, you trust him; and you rejoice with a glorious, inexpressible joy. The reward for trusting him will be the salvation of your souls.
1 Peter 1:6-9 (NLT)

Welcome friend. Today is the day before Thanksgiving here. The time of year that beckons to the front of everyone's mind just what they are thankful for. There is a song I enjoy listening to and the point of the song is that our attitude should be that of gratitude which often is the filter that changes everything.

In Jesus we all have an inexpressible joy. Sometimes that joy encompasses the emotion of happiness and it is easy to express. However, the joy in Christ always runs deeper than that, to the depths of your heart that the emotion of happiness seems to escape, often due to some angle of brokenness in this world.

Dear one, I do not know whether today you are feeling lifted with the easily expressible joy or the inexpressible depth of joy that sustains even still, in the depths of the valley (Psalm 23:4). However I do pray you remember you were made to carry the victory of Christ and that your joy becomes so overflowing from the depths of your heart that you are able to rejoice with a glorious, inexpressible joy.

Let us begin in prayer as we let this one simmer on our heart. May it become the attitude of our mind. *Even though the fig trees have no blossoms, and there are no grapes on the vines; even though the olive crop fails, and the fields lie empty and barren; even though the flocks die in the fields, and the cattle barns are empty, yet I will rejoice in the LORD! I will be joyful in the God of my salvation!* Habakkuk 3:17-18 (NLT) Verse 19 (NLT) begins, *The Sovereign LORD is my strength!*

Wrapped in His sovereign strength let us embark on today's study! We finished yesterday with an in-depth study of John 1:19-28. Today we will examine this event in scripture from different vantage points; Matthew 3:1-12, Mark 1:1-8, and Luke 3:1-18.

Turn to Luke 3:1-18 and take in this event from Luke's perspective. _____

In Luke 3:2 where was John when he received a message from God?

_____

If you feel you are in a "wilderness" season of your life maybe it is just a prepping to receive a wild encounter with God?! Verse 3 (NLT) tells me John was LIVING in the wilderness. The temptation in a wilderness situation or season is to sit idle but might we accept the challenge this verse gives us and LIVE, be ALIVE in the wilderness, it could be around any corner that we find God in need of someone alive and ready to say, *"Here am I, send me!"* (Isaiah 6:8 NIV)

Luke also records John making it clear that he was not the Messiah, the One to come was greater than himself (verse 16). Luke 3:17 records John's message that is quite similar to that of Jesus' in Matthew 25:31-46._____ Read through this passage in Matthew, and you will notice again a calling on all our lives. What do you think it is?

_____

_____

Matthew 25:31-46 gives quite an underlining of the greatest two commandments. Love God and love others. Do we have eyes that see the needs of others? Do we have a heart so full of gratitude for the grace and mercy He has shown us? Are we a willing outsource of that resource toward others? We do not want to be chaff or a goat... and we certainly do not want to end up a chaffed goat! THAT is no pretty picture is it!?!! But I am afraid a chaffed goat is what we look like to others when we fill up on self instead of His Spirit.

1 Corinthians 13:1 (NLT) *If I could speak all the languages of earth and of angels, but didn't love others, I would only be a noisy gong or a clanging cymbal.*

Luke 3:18 (NLT) tells us, *John used many such warnings as he announced the Good News to the people.* 2 Peter 3:9 tells us God is patient but there will come a time when you will have had to have made a choice as to where you want to spend eternity. Continue reading through to 2 Peter 3:10 and we find there is no time like the present, it is a gift, not one of us is guaranteed tomorrow. Decide to side with Christ NOW.

Head over to Matthew 3:1-12 and read those short 12 verses. _____

What is repeated once more that was also stated in both previous passages? (Hint: verse 11)

_____

Someone else is coming who is greater than I.

Mark's gospel account (which we will get to before the day is out) of this scene also records the detail that John clearly made it known that he was not the One but that there was coming One who was much greater than him!

Every one of the gospels records John's humility… it's one thing for one person to see your good side but if EVERYONE around you knows your good side then maybe it's not a side but rather you have allowed an invasion of His Spirit to the point that He seeps out on ALL sides of your life! Hallelujah He is able! Let us not quench His filling. (1 Thess. 5:19)

Back it up to verse 10 in Matthew 3. What kind of fruit is God looking for?

_____

The good kind. What does John 15:4-5 tell us about that?

_____

_____

What is the fruit His Spirit produces? See Galatians 5:22-23

_____

Only in Him will we produce anything worth anything. Is He your vine? Is there anything in your life vying for vine status? See John 10:10.

Be not deceived, there is only one Vine that produces good fruit in our lives and that is our God.

It is not enough to repent of sin, we must then pivot toward God. I like the analogy that a caterpillar can say he is changing but unless he submits to God in the cocoon process he will never really change.

John 13:35 (NLT) states, *Your love for one another will prove to the world that you are my disciples."*

True love is action. We find ourselves back to "loving anyway", and why? Because that is the ultimate way to point to the One who is greater than I/you/us. Loving not with our love but with the love He pours out into us that comes by way of abiding in Him.

Before we wrap up today, we do not want to miss Mark's take. Please read Mark 1:1-8. _____

This is our first glance at the book of Mark so please state below his purpose for writing. (Hint Verse 1)

To share the Good News.

Mark begins his book with the powerful proof of fulfilled Scripture! Mark 1:2-3 can be compared with Isaiah 40:3. Knowing God keeps His promises provides inexplicable comfort.

Psalm 29:11 (NLT) states, *The LORD gives his people strength. The LORD blesses them with peace.* Oh, let's make room to tuck this into your heart's pocket too. (What better way to end a study than a heart full of Truth!)

In Mark 1:4 John preached that baptism was a way to publicly show others they had in a sense put a stake in the ground. An act to stand as a reminder for themselves and others as to Who they were now choosing to live for; the One who gives life and breath to everything and satisfies every need (Acts 17:25).

Mark 1:5 (NLT) states, *All of Judea, including all the people of Jerusalem, went out to see and hear John.* Good night! That is quite a following! Does knowing this explain why ALL four gospel writers included the fact that John continued to point them away from himself and to the One who was greater?! I am sure it was awe inspiring!

The lure of power, fame and wealth can be crippling to any human but to remain, so laser focused when the bait is dangled so within grasp is only the strength of the Holy Spirit. Please record the warning in Mark 4:19 below.

_____

_____

John the Baptist remained humble and thus God was able to do great things through his life to impact the Kingdom. John showed undivided loyalty to God Almighty. When God's name is lifted up what happens? John 12:32 (NLT) holds the answer. *And when I am lifted up from the earth, I will draw everyone to myself."*

Dear one, we don't have to be a professional, or even feel like we are good at it, we just have to be willing to use what He's given us, where He has placed us, and like John the Baptist, continually point to the One who is greater than us. God does the professional work of drawing people into a love relationship with Himself. Praise Him!

So…
- He qualifies whom He calls - His Word is always effective
- Love anyway and with Godly wisdom

- Don't be a chaffed goat

- Remain in the Vine; humble, pliable, submitted to Almighty God, the One far greater than I.

- Our sovereign God knows what He is doing even when it is way beyond our comprehension. *The reward for trusting him will be the salvation of your souls.* 1 Peter 1:9 (NLT)

Goodness, it has been a trip today!! Thank you for being my adventure buddy! Please take a moment before you leave and sort out what He impacted your heart with the most today and record it below as you thank Him for continuing to draw your precious heart into His Almighty one.

_____

_____

_____

_____

Day 4: Plunge Prepared

Hello dear one. Are you ready for today's adventure?! I hope you are wearing your galoshes and have packed your desert terrain hiking boots because we are going ALL over today! Let us pray ourselves up before we get started. In our prayer let's remember the One who guides us is the Lamb who was slain and the Lion who triumphed, He's been through it all and came out the ultimate, eternal, victorious Warrior so we have nothing to fear!

Tuck this into your heart's pocket before we begin: *In a loud voice they were saying: "Worthy is the Lamb, who was slain, to receive power and wealth and wisdom and strength and honor and glory and praise!"* Revelation 5:12 (NIV)

Please start in John 1:29-34 as I think it will be a perfect bridge between where we were yesterday and where we are going today. _____

Once again, we see John the Baptist not miss an opportunity to proclaim to anyone listening that Jesus was greater than him! John knew to the core of his existence that the point of his existence was Jesus!

In this short segment of scripture, it makes it clear that though John was sent to prepare the way for the Messiah he did not know just who he was until God revealed it to him.

Jeremiah 29:13 (NIV) *You will seek me and find me when you seek me with all your heart.* To seek Him with all our heart… think for a moment what that looks like or means to you.

_____

_____

In all I do not know I can trust Him to know and when I need to know He will let me know. What happened that cleared things up for John?
(Hint: verses 32-33)

_____

Now if you remember back in our previous weeks of study, what was the relationship between Jesus and John? *Remember Mary (Jesus' mother) and Elizabeth according to the KJV in Luke 1:36 is Mary's cousin. Remember they spent about three months together just before the birth of John the Baptist. So, this would then make Jesus and John…

_____

Second cousins.

Can you imagine the surprise of John when the Spirit came and rested upon his second cousin!!!?!! Instead of John getting caught up in that he had lived his whole life preparing the way for his cousin… the cousin that he maybe had wrestled with and ate with and now seemed to be THE Messiah!?! John does not fall away on account of God's choice, John does not sit around wallowing in a pity party singing, "why not me…". What is it that he does?

_____

According to John 1:29, 34 (NLT) he says, *"Look! The Lamb of God who takes away the sin of the world! (34) I saw this happen to Jesus, so I testify that he is the Chosen One of God.*

John readily gets behind God's choice, God's way, even when he may not understand it and may have been the farthest thing from what he expected. John continues in humble surrendered service to God Almighty. How are we at responding like John when we find ourselves in situations when we thought God would go right and He went left?

_____

_____

Please read Isaiah 42:1 (NLT) recorded for you below.

"Look at my servant, whom I strengthen. He is my chosen one, who pleases me. I have put my Spirit upon him. He will bring justice to the nations.

It seems to me that John knew the Old Testament enough to be governed by its wisdom. 2 Timothy 3:16-17 (NLT) reminds us, *All Scripture is inspired by God and is useful to teach us what is true and to make us realize what is wrong in our lives. It corrects us when we are wrong and teaches us to do what is right. God uses it to prepare and equip his people to do every good work.*

Becoming familiar with the trustworthy and faithful Word of God can help us remain standing firm in Truth and respond in God honoring ways when we do not quite understand our circumstances.

Please don your galoshes as you wade through Matthew 3:13-17. _____

Just something super cool: In Matthew 3:16-17 we see evidence of the Trinity. Our God is three in one. Sort of like an eggshell, egg yolk and the egg white, for a simple illustration. All three parts make up the same egg as a whole. You cannot have the whole without each part. Here in our passage, Jesus, God the Son is baptized, God the Holy Spirit descends like a dove, and God the Father speaks. I am so glad there are incomprehensible mysteries of God! They just remind me that He is able to handle all the things in my life that are so way beyond my ability to shoulder and comprehend. Praise Him!

In Matthew 3:14 what is it that John asks Jesus?

_____

Why are You coming to me?

I wonder if we have ever asked God the same question and if not verbally at least implied it with our actions?

"Why are you coming to me God?! I'm too busy. Can't you see I'm serving you so much already doing this thing over here?!!" OR "Why are you coming to me God, so and so would be SOOOO much better at this than I!"

If God has come to us might we humbly submit not only to His reasoning but to His will and way which will always be beyond us in ourselves alone and that is why He is Immanuel, God with us. Always (Matthew 28:20)!

It would appear in our passage that John is feeling unqualified to do what Jesus has asked of him. Have you ever felt unqualified in a position you found yourself in? How did it play out?

_____

_____

John voices his concern to Jesus and what is Jesus' response in Matthew 3:15?

_____

...we must carry out all that God requires. (NLT) They were able to look back at the Old Testament Scriptures and see that the whole thing foreshadows and points forward to the coming of Christ. Jesus knew the Word and thus knew what He was to fulfill. Reading the Word gives our lives meaning, purpose and clarity.

Micah 6:8 (NIV) tells us what is required of us. *He has shown you, O mortal, what is good. And what does the LORD require of you? To act justly and to love mercy and to walk humbly with your God.*

Please read Jeremiah 31:31-34 to catch a glimpse of what Jesus knew was required of Him.

Now jog over to Galatians in the New Testament and read chapter 3:6-14.
_____

Between these two passages from the Old Testament and the New we gather that Jesus knew He was bringing the new covenant. Abraham long ago had been called by God and given a promise by God Himself that all nations would be blessed through Him (Genesis 12:1-3). One day Jesus would come through his line and through the Son of God's death on the cross and resurrection we would all be blessed!

All those who believe will be given the Holy Spirit to live by, freeing us from the law that was given to Moses by God years and years after Abraham received the promise. The finger of God that first chose to write His Word on tablets of stone (Ex. 31:18) wants to remove our heart of stone and give us a heart of flesh (Ez. 36:26) able to truly receive His living Word straight onto the tablet of our hearts!

The law was useful and given to preserve us until Christ came to save us. The law proved we were unable to earn salvation on our own. None could keep the law to perfection, we needed a Savior and Jesus is it. Now those of us who believe have the empowering of His Spirit within us to help us live according to His Word. He reminds us of the instructions written deep within our hearts and helps us in our time of temptation and need, reminding us of His grace, forgiveness and redeeming power when we sin.

Matthew 3:15 records that John, in all his feelings of insufficient qualifications again submitted to God. John asked a question… Why me?! And Jesus pointed him to the Scriptures that must be fulfilled, and it was enough for John to step forward in faith. Is it enough for you?

Now to view this scenario from Marks vantage point let us wade on over to Mark 1:9-11. _____

I love that Mark begins verse 9 (NLT) with, *One day*, what a spectacular day it turned out to be but when it began it was just "one day". Are we living ready every day because one day Jesus will return for us?!

Matthew 24:36 (NLT) *"However, no one knows the day or hour when these things will happen, not even the angels in heaven or the Son himself. Only the Father knows.*

Before we close for the day, wade on over to see this from Luke's vantage point in chapter 3:21-22. _____

Verse 21 (NLT) *One day when the crowds were being baptized, Jesus himself was baptized. As he was praying, the heavens opened,*
Please circle "when the crowds" and "Jesus himself". Do you know that right there amid a crowd, Jesus stands WITH you, He stands FOR you dear one?!

In that same verse 21 printed out for you, please underline "As he was praying" and box "the heavens opened". Do you believe in the power of prayer? Romans 12:12 (NIV) encourages us to be faithful in prayer. *Be joyful in hope, patient in affliction, faithful in prayer.* 1 Thessalonians 5:17 (NIV) tells us to, *pray continually.* Please fill in the blanks below according to the last part of James 5:16 (NIV).

The prayer of a righteous person is _____ *and* _____. (powerful, effective)

James 5:17-18 (NIV) *Elijah was a human being, even as we are. He prayed earnestly that it would not rain, and it did not rain on the land for three and a half years. Again he prayed, and the heavens gave rain, and the earth produced its crops.*

Alright my friend before you switch to our desert terrain boots let's make camp here and allow His all sufficient, fully equipping Word of Truth to wash over us and soak up in all the places we didn't even know were dry.

Please record the most impacting point that God made to your heart today.

_____

_____

_____

_____

Day 5: Purified Like Silver

Hi friend! I hope you have packed up those galoshes from our quest through Scripture yesterday and are ready with those desert hiking boots! It might get a bit wild today, watch out for snakes! Any good adventure must begin in prayer, so I will meet you after that and on the other side of our three passages listed below.

Please read Mark 1:12-13 _____., Matthew 4:1-11 _____, and Luke 4:1-13. _____

I was afraid that the tempter had gotten the best of you (1 Thessalonians 3:5 NLT).

Good golly can we pray for ourselves and for our loved ones and for our leaders and really, probably every breathing soul could stand to be included in the prayer that God help us not let the tempter get the best of us!!! Not get the best of our marriages and friendships, families and endeavors! Do not let the enemy get the best of your ideas, plans, vacations… commit to the Lord all that you are, all that you do, and recommit as many times as it takes!

How do we not let the enemy get the best of us?! We make the Lord our Vine; we remain in Him and when we slip, we get back up EVERY TIME and turn back to God. The best is still in His hand dear one!

We can pray part of 1 Chronicles 29:19 (NLT) (below) and insert in the "my son Solomon" part with your own scenarios to make it more personal so that in all we do we work ultimately to wholeheartedly "build" to and for His glory and praise.

Give my son Solomon the wholehearted desire to obey all your commands, laws, and decrees, and to do everything necessary to build this Temple,

Looking first at Mark 1:12-13 as that is the shortest recording in the gospels of the temptation of Jesus after His baptism, not without great impact for sure. Mark 1:11 records Jesus just having experienced a superb moment! He hears the voice of God the Father from heaven stating that He brings Him great joy and that He is dearly loved! The very next verse (12) tells us the Spirit compelled Jesus to go into the wilderness! What?! Now why would that happen?!

Just because you find yourself in a desert wilderness situation does not mean you have done wrong. Although God never tempts someone to do wrong, He may allow it in order to strengthen your stance for Him. Remember He never sends you somewhere alone and He always provides a way out of temptation so that you can be successful over it.

James 1:13 (NIV) *because you know that the testing of your faith produces perseverance.*

1 Corinthians 10:13 (NIV) *No temptation has overtaken you except what is common to mankind. And God is faithful; he will not let you be tempted beyond what you can bear. But when you are tempted, he will also provide a way out so that you can endure it.*
I think it might be like this… (the following may or may not be a personal experience…) I can run every day on a treadmill and be just fine but then one

day I think I'm so in shape I'll just go ahead and do the same workout time on the elliptical... only to find out to my horror the next day that EVERY single muscle in my "in shape" body is screaming, "You are NOT AT ALL in as good of shape as you THOUGHT girlfriend!!"

The times we are allowed to go through an exercise that is uncomfortable it may be to strengthen parts of our faith that we had no idea needed strengthening. Please read Job 23:10-12 and record how it impacts your heart below.

_____

_____

Mark 1:13 indicates Jesus was out among what?

_____

What kind of "wild animals" do you face daily? Are there any that you have been around so long that you no longer see as "wild"? Have you become so accustomed to them that they appear tame? How might we get back our sensitivity to that which we have become desensitized to by this world's worldliness?

_____

_____

_____

_____

Please read Romans 12:2, Hebrews 4:15, 1 Thessalonians 5:17 and record the impact you feel on your heart below.

_____

_____

Now let us compare Matthew 4:1-11 and Luke 4:1-13 as they have both recorded these events similarly.

There are three temptations, please list them in the order they appear in Matthew and then in Luke. (Hint look around... Matt. 4:3,6,9 and Luke 4:3,7,9)

Matthew	Luke

I see that both list the temptation to eat bread after Jesus has not eaten in 40 days, listed first in each gospel. Of all things out there to eat the enemy had to use bread! I find bread to be an endless temptation no matter when I last ate!!! He didn't use eggplant or something… all though even eggplant after 40 days would start lookin' good probably! The enemy tempts with what he knows has the highest probability to work or, not being highly creative, will use something that has worked in the past. May we be wise to the enemy's schemes!

1 Peter 5:8 (NLT) *Stay alert! Watch out for your great enemy, the devil. He prowls around like a roaring lion, looking for someone to devour.*

The second temptations are listed in a different order between the two gospels of Matthew and Luke. Matthew lists the enemy tempting Jesus to test God, to just jump off the highest point of the Temple. Luke lists the second temptation as the offer from the enemy to get the authority and glory from all the kingdoms of the world.

The enemy is tempting Jesus to bypass God's way. Jesus is King of kings and Lord of lords and one day every knee in heaven and on earth will bow but God said it would be by way of the cross. The enemy is trying to tempt Jesus to get the glory without the cross. But if Jesus had given in, all would have been lost!

Matthew 7:15 (NLT) *"Beware of false prophets who come disguised as harmless sheep but are really vicious wolves.* John 10:10 tells us the enemy comes only to steal, kill and destroy. If the enemy can't get you to end your own life one way or another he will try and get you to buy into the world's way of self-honoring fame, power and money which guarantees sure death! *What good is it for someone to gain the whole world, yet forfeit their soul?* Mark 8:36 (NIV)

What is it that makes Jesus withstand the enemy each time he comes at Him?

Scripture! We must know the Word of Truth!! We must know it so well that when the enemy twists Truth into a lie we recognize it and call his bluff straight out!!

"Get behind me, Satan! You are a stumbling block to me; you do not have in mind the concerns of God, but merely human concerns." Matthew 16:23 (NIV)

Submit yourselves, then, to God. Resist the devil, and he will flee from you. James 4:7 (NIV)

Luke 4:13 indicates that the devil finished tempting Jesus and left him until when?

You are important to God and that means the enemy is in hot pursuit of you and is always on the prowl for an opportune time to come at you again. Be on your guard.

As we close please look back at what John called Jesus in John 1:29.

"Look! The Lamb of God who takes away the sin of the world! (NLT)

The Lamb that was slain became the Lion that triumphed! (Revelation 5:5-9)

You have given me your shield of victory. Your right hand supports me; your help has made me great. Psalm 18:35 (NLT)

In Ephesians 6:16 the shield in the armor of God is faith! It is steadfast faith that extinguishes all the flaming arrows of the evil one! Keep the faith in Jesus the Lamb of God who has purified you from all unrighteousness and has set you free, do not let the enemy put chains on you!

As we close please savor Psalm 66 and praise Him for the times as verse 10 indicates, *You have tested us, O God; you have purified us like silver.* (NLT)

Thank you dear one for today, may we leave filled up, to be sent out, in order to come back, praising Him stronger than ever; refined in the fire!

Please record what God has impacted your heart with the most today.

_____

_____

_____

_____

Day 6 & 7: At His Feet – A Time to Reflect

Over the next two days take time to reflect over your week of study. Maybe you need some time to catch up on the study material and this might be the perfect break to do just that with the Lord!

I encourage you to glance back at the final point at the end of each day that you recorded having had the greatest impact on your heart. As you spend time with God in prayer, reflect and record on the lines below how God is tying it together and applying it to your life specifically for such a time as this.

Ask that God make it clear who He would have you invite into an opportunity to share Him, to apply what you are learning; maybe a child, grandchild, friend… trust Him to continue to take the lead. May we have a heart ever ready with eyes and ears out to the opportunities God wants to invite us into for His glory and praise.

Do not merely listen to the word, and so deceive yourselves. Do what it says. Anyone who listens to the word but does not do what it says is like someone who looks at his face in a mirror and, after looking at himself, goes away and immediately forgets what he looks like. But whoever looks intently into the perfect law that gives freedom, and continues in it – not forgetting what they have heard, but doing it – they will be blessed in what they do.
James 1:22-25 (NIV)

_____

_____

_____

_____

_____

_____

_____

_____

Philippians 4:13 (NIV) *I can do all this through him who gives me strength.*

John 14:26 (NIV) *But the Advocate, the Holy Spirit, whom the Father will send in my name, will teach you all things and will remind you of everything I have said to you.*

WEEK 5
Taste and see that the LORD is good; blessed is the one who takes refuge in him.
Psalm 34:8 (NIV)

Day 1: Come and See
Hello my friend. Today we will be uncovering in Scripture just a few of the many reasons to follow our Lord and Savior Jesus Christ. Let us first bow before Him praising Him that He himself gives life and breath to everything and satisfies every need (Acts 17:25). We all have need of the great I Am, the Lamb of God, Immanuel who gives us strength and peace (Psalm 29:11). May He lead us this day to be ever more deeply in love with His heart, revealing great and unsearchable things we do not know (Jer. 33:3). Alright my friend, come and see with me!

Beginning in John 1:35, please continue reading through verse 51. _____

Taking it from the beginning we see in John 1:36 John is recorded lifting up the name of God as what again?

_____

The Lamb of God.

When John does this what happens? (Hint: verse 37)

_____

John's disciples left to follow Jesus! John does not go jealously running after them, he lets them go, as this is an example of the purpose of our very existence! Our lives are to lift up His name. John 12:32 (NASB) reminds us, *"And I, if I am lifted up from the earth, will draw all men to Myself."*

Jesus wonders what these two former disciples of John are wanting and what do the disciples ask Jesus in John 1:38?

"where are you staying?" (NIV)

Have you ever wanted to ask Jesus that? "Where are you staying, God? I mean I see You moving here and there and in that, but where are You staying so I can just plan on where I can settle and set up camp?!" "I want to know where Your base camp is God so I can know if it's too far or if I think I can make it." Except how do we see Jesus answer these two fellows within verse 39?

"Come and see," (NLT)

It is not about the destination as much as it is the journey. In Jesus we know the destination - heaven. If we can let go of always looking to the next "rest stop" we might just enjoy the adventure in the step we are currently in! We might see Him that much more if we are looking for Him in our step rather than for the next stop. Honestly if we would relax a bit, we would realize He is ever with us in our rests, steps and stops!!

In John 1:41 what does Andrew do upon finding out Jesus is the Messiah?

I love Andrew for this! He has a heart to bring people to Jesus! In the parable of the five loaves and two fish that feeds 5,000 that we will study later, it is again Andrew that brings the little boy with that small lunch to Jesus! (John 6:8-9)

How readily do you introduce people to Jesus? When there is a problem or someone you know has a problem, how quickly does your brain default to knowing all answers are found in Jesus and going to Him is your first plan of action? How would you rate yourself on a scale from 1-10, 1 being you always go to Him first?

1 2 3 4 5 6 7 8 9 10

John 1:42 informs us that Jesus gives Simon a new name. What is it?

Simon is not always pictured in Scripture for his wise choices. Often Scripture paints him in all honesty, including his shortcomings, failings and I personally am so very glad of that because Jesus still labels Simon with hope"Simon is well known in the Gospels, not for his courage and faith, but for his failings (see 18:15-18, 25-27). Jesus named him Cephas ("the rock"; see 1:42), referring to the great church leader he would later become (Acts 1:1-5:42; 8:1-12:25; 15:1-41)."[vii]

Revelation 2:17 NIV *Whoever has ears, let them hear what the Spirit says to the churches. To the one who is victorious, I will give some of the hidden manna. I will also give that person a white stone with a new name written on it, known only to the one who receives it.*

We in Jesus will receive a new name. Often a name represents the character of the person who holds it. As Jesus gave Simon a new name, Cephas or Peter, Jesus was calling him for who He purposed him to be, for who He knew his true identity to be, in Him.

People look at the outward appearance, but the LORD looks at the heart." (1 Sam. 16:7 NIV)

The Lord sees the real you dear one. He sees who He purposed you to be and with your lungs still breathing and heart still beating, He proves He still believes it to hold true of you. Let the Truth that God states about you ring loudest in your mind and heart.

How might we raise the volume on the Truth God speaks over another's life? Our own life?

_____

_____

When Jesus called Simon, Peter (the rock), Simon was acting… well let us just say not so rock like at times. Sometimes we must choose to see what God sees, believe all things are possible with God. Then a step in that direction becomes easier until one day you have become just who God said you were all along!

John 1:43 tells us Jesus finds who?

Philip

God calls a heart and sometimes He does it through "Andrew's" but every time He does it through His Word. Romans 10:17 (NIV) *Consequently, faith comes from hearing the message, and the message is heard through the word about Christ.*

Remember back to our first week of study… (John 1:1) - the Word is God. The Word found Philip and what was the message (verse 43)?

"Come, follow me." (NLT)

Come follow the Lamb of God, the Savior, the God with you - Immanuel, the God who gives you a new name and redeems your soul… come see for yourself… come follow Me… Jesus calls to all of us. John 3:16 (NIV) *For God so loved the world that he gave his one and only Son, that whoever believes in him shall not perish but have eternal life.*

By John 1:45 who is Philip going to bring to Jesus?

Nathaniel! When the Word gets into your heart you cannot contain it!! Psalm 107:2 (NIV) *Let the redeemed of the LORD tell their story* -- Jeremiah 20:9 (NIV) *But if I say, "I will not mention his word or speak anymore in his name," his word is in my heart like a fire, a fire shut up in my bones. I am weary of holding it in; indeed, I cannot.*

In John 1:46 we see Nathaniel respond in a bit of disbelief; to which Philip responds with what familiar phrase?

"Come and see," (NIV)

Sometimes all we need to invite people to do is to "come and see" for themselves. If someone genuinely wants to find the Lord, He will be found by them. Jeremiah 29:13 (NIV) *You will seek me and find me when you seek me with all your heart.*

What question does Nathaniel ask Jesus in verse 48?

"How do you know about me?" (NIV)

Have you ever been tempted to ask God the same question? "How do you know about me God?" or maybe even, "DO you know about me?!" The more we understand WHO He is the more obvious the answer to that question becomes.

We see Jesus answers Nathaniel with information about himself that astounds Nathaniel. Only God Almighty could know that about him!

Let us look at some Scripture that will blow our minds on what only God Almighty could know about us. Please read the following scriptures and record what each says He knows about you. The first one is done for you in the following chart.

Jeremiah 29:11	He knows the good plans for your life.
Luke 12:7	
Psalm 139:4, 13-14, 16-17	
Psalm 56:8	
Acts 17:26	

Amazing! Only our Creator God!

Jesus expounds on Nathaniel's amazement with how God knew about him, to reveal an even greater Truth. What does Jesus reveal about Himself in John 1:51?

_____

_____

Jesus reveals He is the Ladder the Stairway (Thus fulfilling Genesis 28:12), the only Way to heaven from earth! Nathaniel asks, "How do you know me?" and Jesus in a sense says, "How could I NOT know about you?! I love you!! I am the Way for you to be with me always for eternity!"

When you are tempted to feel like you are lost in all oblivion remember He knows the way that you take, He knows the plans for you, He knows the hairs on your head and the number of tears you have cried, He knit you together and is the ladder between heaven and earth for you. He came down from on high to be the Way back to Him for all eternity! You are not oblivious but rather obviously… loved!

In Genesis 28:1-17 when the ladder or stairway between heaven and earth is first mentioned, Jacob says in verse 16 (NLT*) *"Surely the LORD is in this place, and I wasn't even aware of it!"*

Dear one, the Lord is in your place, in your situation, He sees you! God promises to be working all things together for good for those that love Him (Romans 8:28) even when you cannot see how. Why? Because He loves you.

Please record the most profound point God made on your heart today.

_____
_____
_____
_____

Day 2: What's Your Fuel?

Welcome beloved of God. Let us jump right on in today as I believe God has something purely amazing for us to see! Be sure to bow in prayer asking for eyes to see like His and ears to hear as He hears and especially for a heart willing to be obedient to what He reveals.

Tucking this one in my heart right now! Matthew 13:16 (NIV) *But blessed are your eyes because they see, and your ears because they ear.*

Please read John 2:1-12. _____

In John 2:3 how does Jesus' mother present the problem to Him?

_____

She states it. She does not offer Him suggestions on how she thinks He should fix it. Mary leaves the problem in His hands and tells the servants what, in verse 5?

"Do whatever he tells you." (NIV) So even if He does not want you to do anything then that is the direction to follow. Proverbs 3:6 (NIV) *in all your ways submit to him, and he will make your paths straight.*

Sometimes the hardest directives to follow involve a standstill, am I right?!! Can you share a time when you submitted your way to His? How did things work out?

_____

_____

_____

When Jesus works the miracle at this wedding who does verse 9 indicate knew about what had been done?

_____

Again, like His birth announcement when the first to know were the lowly shepherds, it is the servants that are the first to know about His first miracle!

How does this contrast this worlds value system that places so much importance on power and prestige?

_____

In what ways have we allowed this world's value system to influence us?

_____

_____

Are the motives behind who you reveal the events in your life, governed by a heart of sincerity and truth? This may be a question we need to submit to God for the whole truth in every area of our lives to come to light - in all honesty. Please read Matthew 6:3-4 ___ before responding. You may even just want to record a prayer to God asking that He reveal your motives and that in all situations He be the purifier of them so that He is what fuels them.

_____

_____

_____

John 2:10 indicates the perplexing situation that the best wine had been saved for last - how uncommon! The blessing of this was unexpected and more than they could have asked for.

Have you received a blessing so unexpected and yet so much more wonderful than you could have ask for?

_____

_____

I think Jesus is that blessing for all of us. So much more wonderful than we could have ever hoped for.

Please read further into John chapter 2, verses 13-25. _____

Here we see God's passion explode! John 2:17 records the disciples making sense of His actions by remembering what?

_____

_____

A prophecy in Scripture! (See Psalm 69:9.)

When we do not understand what God is doing search the Scriptures. He aligns with His Word 100% of the time. Praise Him!

When we feel our passion ready to explode might we check ourselves and make sure that what ignites our passion is what would ignite His. Again, remember and measure all against His faithful Word.

In John 2:18 the Jewish leaders asked a question. What was it?

_____

"What are you doing? (NLT)

I am sure many of us have wanted to ask God this same question. What does Jesus answer them with in verse 19?

_____

Verses 21 explains His answer, so what was Jesus really pointing them to when He answered their question (verse 22)?

_____

_____

When we want to ask, "What are you doing Lord?" Maybe we need to remember what He has already done, what He has already told us. Like the disciples needed to do, maybe we need to look to the cross and the empty tomb. Remembering He loved us so much He gave His life for all humanity and overcame the grave!

Please read 1 Corinthians 15:55-57 with rejoicing that He is our Living Hope! We can look the world over and we will find nothing that fuels our hearts like the Living Hope of our God!

Thank you for your diligent study. Please record below that which made the most impact on your heart today.

_____
_____
_____
_____

Day 3: Again?!

Thank you sincerely for meeting me here AGAIN! You have completed over an entire month of in-depth Bible study! Well done! *Anyone who wants to be my disciple must follow me, because my servants must be where I am. And the Father will honor anyone who serves me.* John 12:26 (NLT)

Wow! How good is our God that He honors His servants!! The God to whom we owe our every breath, to whom we owe are very life, *deserves* our service! What an honor to even be called His servant AND YET He says He will *honor* His servants! All the time our God is oh so, so good! Let us praise Him in prayer as we begin.

A particular meeting in the night between Jesus and a man named Nicodemus is where we will start. Please read John 3:1-21. ____

In John 3:4 Nicodemus asks Jesus what He means by being born AGAIN?! Jesus takes the time to explain things to Him and still Nicodemus can't quite wrap his head around the answer and in verse 9 (NLT) asks, *"How are these things possible?"*

Do you have questions about what Jesus means exactly? I mean, you get an answer but you just wrestle with how it can/could all be possible?! Go ahead and write what is on your heart if you have something.

_____

_____

Jesus was trying to explain to Nicodemus that you cannot get into the Kingdom by just living a good life, you need to be spiritually reborn. Jesus elaborates in verse 14. Jesus makes an analogy here for Nicodemus with an event that Nicodemus would have been familiar with recorded in the Old Testament (Numbers 21:8-9). Jesus then states His "why" in John 3:15 (NLT) *so that everyone who believes in him will have eternal life.*

Breaking down the teaching method: First Jesus addresses the wrong way of thinking - being good is not enough because we can never be good enough.

Next Jesus relates His answer to something Nicodemus could remember and find familiar to create an understandable frame of reference.

Finally, Jesus states His answer in the simplest of terms - believe in Me as God and Savior - John 3:16 - that is how you make it to the Kingdom.

When we are finding it hard to understand what God means, look to His Word to find out Truth. Knowing Truth will expose the lie.

Remember Who He is in His Word, remember His faithfulness to you in the past (Hebrews 13:8). Allow this to form a frame of reference. Then drop your anchor of trust so that you are not tossed about in the waves of doubt.

Look to the cross and remember His love that has saved your life, has rescued you for all eternity to be with Him in paradise. *"There is no judgement against anyone who believes in him.* (John 3:18 NLT)

Choose to receive His gift of peace that surpasses understanding; to take to heart all that we DO know, and lay to rest all that we DON'T, in the trusted hand of Who we know does.

If our questions keep us close to God than I believe we have already received an answer far beyond what we imagined.

Please rest in the Truths of Philippians 4:7 (NIV) *And the peace of God, which transcends all understanding, will guard your hearts and your minds in Christ Jesus.* and 1 Corinthians 13:12 (NIV) *For now we see only a reflection as in a mirror; then we shall see face to face. Now I know in part; then I shall know fully, even as I am fully known.*

In closing I pray you have come to see over this week that…

- He is the God who is not afraid of questions, Who invites us to "come and see", to walk with Him in relationship.

- He is the God who looks at the heart and calls you by your true name.

- He is the God that is your ladder, your Way to heaven. He is the One who invented passion and knows how to correctly use it.

- He is love and He loves you and wants you and wants you to invite others to "come and see" again and again and again that He is the Way, the Truth and the Life for all who would believe in Jesus as Savior! (John 14:6)

Please take a moment to record the thing that God used to make the biggest impact on your heart today. God bless you muchly and see you AGAIN soon!

_____
_____
_____
_____

Day 4: Found, Follow, Find

Hi there beloved of God. If I am this grateful to have you spending time in His Word with me can you just imagine the Father's delight in your diligence to pursue His heart?!! Zephaniah 3:17 (NIV) states, *The LORD your God is with you, the Mighty Warrior who saves. He will take great delight in you; in his love he will no longer rebuke you but will rejoice over you with singing."* Rejoice over you! What a delight to think that the Creator God delights over us with singing!!!! Let us praise Him for being such a good, good Father and ask that He faithfully take the lead of our hearts journey into His today.

We will pick up where we left off in our reading yesterday. Please read John 3:22-4:3. _____

Before we embark on our journey too far today please tuck this part of John 3:27 (NLT) in your heart's pocket. *"No one can receive anything unless God gives it from heaven.*

John 3:23 indicates John the Baptist was baptizing at Aenon, near Salim, why?

_____

This seems like such a simple and random piece of information however how often have we over complicated things with trying to discern the will of God? John found a place to carry out God's will for his life simply because there was provision of water and people. John didn't get wrapped up in the level of the water or the quality of the water or the number of people - there was water, there was a person - there was the call to baptize - and so he did. Is there anything you are overcomplicating in your life?

_____

(Personally, I might need more than just one line to record the number of things I tend to overanalyze in life! Sorry, complete work-in-progress over here!)

How might we follow John's example in Jesus and keep it simple? Maybe we are to be doing what we can, with what we have, right where we are at. If God wanted John to baptize elsewhere, I am sure God would have made that clear. God desires for us to know and do His will so I highly doubt He would hide it and make sure it was impossible to find! If we are walking with Him in close relationship and making Him the desire of our hearts, He will lead us in His will. Please record below Proverbs 3:5-6.

_____

_____

_____

Now what issue seems to arise in John 3:26 that does not seem to ruffle John's feathers, but it sure does those around him?!

_____

_____

John has never lost sight of his purpose, the point of his existence and ours is Jesus. John can stay above the comparison game because his validation and motivation come from the Father. Where does yours come from?

_____

God has created many people and many people may do the same job, but believe me as no two fingerprints are the same, God uses each individual willing to turn their gifts and talents back to Him for His glory, effectively for His Kingdom. Please record Ephesians 2:10 below.

_____

_____

When you work for the praise of God rather than the praise of people you are set free! What does James 3:16 remind us we never want to be part of?

_____

_____

John the Baptist remains undivided in loyalty to God Almighty. In John 3:28 (NLT) it records once again John saying, *'I am not the Messiah. I am only here to prepare the way for him.'* John is simply glad to stand with Him… he is filled with joy at the success of Jesus. In verse 30 John reiterates, *He must become greater and greater, and I must become less and less.*

Living your life, using your ability, in the slice of pie He has assigned to you for such a time as this for His glory will afford you much more joy than constantly vying for that which you think you want and has been assigned to someone else! There is freedom in celebrating the successes of others and simple gladness to be had in knowing you stand with God on the side of victory!

John had fulfilled his purpose, the way for Jesus had been prepared and people had now found the Messiah and were following Him! What joy! As John 3:36 (NLT) starts out, *And anyone who believes in God's Son has eternal life.*

3 John 1:4 (NIV) *I have no greater joy than to hear that my children are walking in the truth.*

Who has God given you to prepare the way to Him for? Who is in your circle of influence? Without overcomplicating things, what do you have that you can do/use right where you are to impact others with His love? Don't look around and compare with what others are doing, *Look to the LORD and his strength; seek his face always.* Psalm 105:4 (NIV)

_____

Before we wrap up today you won't want to miss the gem in these last few short passages found in Luke 3:19-20 _____, Matthew 4:12 _____ and Mark 1:14. _____

John continued to stand for Truth and what happened in Luke 3:19-20?

_____

John was arrested yet what continued in Mark 1:14?

_____

2 Timothy 2:8-9 (NIV) *Remember Jesus Christ, raised from the dead, descended from David. This is my gospel, for which I am suffering even to the point of being chained like a criminal. But God's word is not chained.*

Praise that our God has overcome!! There are no chains on Him nor on His Word! There are no chains on His beloved child that He has not overcome! Dear one if you did not know Him before this study, I pray you have found Him here and will choose to trust His Truth and receive His free gift of eternal life. John 8:36 (NIV) *So if the Son sets you free, you will be free indeed.*

Know we have not seen the end of John just yet in our study and we can't call it an end to our day until we have sat with our Lord and asked just what He wants our hearts to remember to live forward in Him. Please record that which held the greatest impact for you below.

_____
_____
_____
_____

Thank you ~ As you seek to follow Him more closely may you find the grace, peace, joy and living hope that can only be found in Him. God bless you.

Day 5: Carry Contrast

Dear beloved of God, I am so incredibly grateful that God has stirred our hearts up to pursue Him with diligence and that we have found ourselves landing on the same page again to continue our study! This is answered prayer for sure so let us take a moment to thank Him and praise Him that He is able to keep us strong to the end (1 Cor. 1:8)!

Now dear one, *May the Lord direct your hearts to the love of God and to the steadfastness of Christ.* 2 Thessalonians 3:5 (ESV) and while we are at it let us just stick that verse as a prayer in our heart's pocket!

We previously read about a man named Nicodemus, today we will begin with a young woman at a well. These two stand in complete contrast to one another.

Please begin today in Mark 1:14-15 ____, and Matthew 4:12-17 ____.
In Mark we pick up exactly where we left off. Remember who is in prison?

_____

Where does this passage in Mark indicate Jesus went to preach?

_____

Galilee: however, in John's gospel (which we will get to in a moment) we will get to catch a glimpse of what happens along the way!

Have you ever been too caught up in a destination that you missed the beauty of opportunity along the way?

_____

_____

What might we do in order to slow down and be more intentional about the journey? In my purse I carry a supply of dum-dum suckers. Why? Well, I have six children and somewhere along the way I figured out that carrying a stash of sweets for the journey often makes the journey well, um, sweeter!

What do you have inside you that could be shared to make the journey sweeter? God is always available first thing in the morning to fill up our "purses" with all the sweetness we will need for the day's journey. Do we take enough time with Him so that He can fill us with exactly what only He knows we need that day; not just to make it to the destination but to do the journey well; to make it sweeter for someone else just by being on the path?!

_____

_____

Satisfy us in the morning with your unfailing love, that we may sing for joy and be glad all our days. Psalm 90:14 (NIV) "Joy is the conscious presence of Jesus in your soul." - Jill Briscoe

In our Matthew 4:12-17 passage we again see Jesus begins teaching as John's time ends. When something ends do you automatically lean toward trust and looking to see the new beginning God is working out or is panic and freak out mode the default?

_____

_____

When something ends God is not scrambling around like it caught Him by surprise, He is never without a plan and remains the Source of all resources to carry His plan to completion, 100%, no loose ends. Trust Him, *But Jesus replied, "My Father is always working, and so am I."* John 5:17 (NLT)

Matthew 4:14 indicates that Jesus' move fulfilled Scripture. Isaiah 9:1-2 is Matthew 4:15-16. It would seem Jesus followed the Scriptures like a road map. Remember what Proverbs 3:5-6 (NIV) tells us? *Trust in the LORD with all your heart and lean not on your own understanding; in all your ways submit to him, and he will make your paths straight.*

Jesus is the Word. Know the Word and Trust the Word. He will not lead you astray. Walk with Him in a relationship as I know we are both trying to do as we have come thus far in this study of Him. *Those who honor me I will honor* (1 Sam. 2:30 NIV).

Remember back in Matthew 2:22-23, Jesus' father Joseph was warned in a dream to escape harm and go to Galilee. Jesus too, could have been guarded against possible harm after His friend John the Baptist was arrested as He followed what He knew in the Word. Maybe it's a feeling of uneasiness pricked by the Holy Spirit within you or direct instruction from His written Word… However, God chooses to speak to your heart, John 10:27 (NIV) tells us, *My sheep listen to my voice; I know them, and they follow me.* Isaiah 30:21 (NIV) *Whether you turn to the right or the left, your ears will hear a voice behind you, saying, "This is the way; walk in it."* It does not say the way will be easy, but we will not be alone, the great I AM all we could ever need, will be with us, close enough to hear His loving whisper.

In making decisions I find going back to what I know, to be helpful. Going back to when it did make sense and working from there. Praying and reading His Word continually until I feel His leading. It may be "wait" or "no" but praying against allowing my own wants to cloud my judgement and seeking wise counsel. Making sure to always align the "wise counsel" up with the Word because there is no wiser counsel than from The Wonderful Counselor (Isaiah 9:6).

If we seek Him with all our heart and get no clear negative and we step forward, but it ends up not right, we must trust that He is big enough to use our mistake for His glory. (Romans 8:28)

Never forget on the journey, He is FOR you not against you. Remember we said that Matthew 4:15-16 references Isaiah 9:1-2. The passage in Matthew references "Galilee of the Gentiles" (ESV) and Isaiah references "Galilee of the nations" (ESV). Jesus launched a WORLDWIDE mission… the Good News of Jesus Christ and the Kingdom was not just for the Jews but is for ALL people that would believe!!

Turn now to see how one gal was able to learn from her mistakes and move forward into what was still, GREAT purpose for her life in Him! Please read John 4:4-42 _____.

Recall our passage on Nicodemus (John 3:1-21). This story of the Samaritan woman at the well contrasts Nicodemus' at every turn! First, she was a woman not a man and an outcast Samaritan not a highly respected Jewish religious leader like Nicodemus. However, despite all that she seemed to fall short in, according to the world's standards, who of the two actually RESPONDED to the words of Jesus?

_____

Nicodemus seems to have fallen silent in John 3 however the Samaritan woman shamelessly shares her simple testimony and transforms a village in favor of the Kingdom!

How willing are you to allow Jesus to invade your life? To invoke a transformation within you that creates such a contrast to the world that people cannot help but take notice and praise God?

_____

Finally, dear brothers and sisters, we ask you to pray for us. Pray that the Lord's message will spread rapidly and be honored wherever it goes, just as when it came to you. 2 Thessalonians 3:1 (NLT)

Will you underline "spread rapidly and be honored" in the above verse. May we make this a prayer, that God's Word in us, His message, would spread rapidly and be honored everywhere it went!

After John is arrested Jesus leaves Judea and travels to Galilee however unlike the majority who commonly traveled the longer route to avoid the outcast Samaritan people Jesus took the direct route trekking straight through Samaria!

That may have seemed appalling to most at the time but how different are we now?! Jesus Christ gave up heaven to come to earth and save us yet still we have the audacity to point fingers at the "Samaritans" and accuse them of _____ (we could all fill in that blank with self-righteous judgment) when in reality we were ALL outcasts, EVERY SINGLE ONE of us until Jesus came to our "Samaria" heart and redeemed us from the destination of hell though His sacrifice and resurrection! Oh, praise Him for His redeeming grace!!!

What are you doing specifically to lay aside judgment, still holding to Truth, but in love? The end part of Galatians 5:6 (NIV) is encouraging. *The only thing that counts is faith expressing itself through love.*

_____

Jesus invaded this earth with His love. We who believe in Him have received the invasion of His Holy Spirit within us! Please read 2 Corinthians 4:7-11 and respond with how you, as His vessel, His jar of clay, take hold of the treasure within you? How do you show the all-surpassing power of Him within you to love, give mercy and grace, to forgive, to hold your tongue to respond in gentleness…?

_____

_____

_____

Paul tells us in 2 Corinthians 6:4-5, 11:23-28 and 1 Corinthians 4:10-13 about a number of hardships he faced yet at every turn he remained rooted in Christ, exemplifying the fruit of the Spirit (Gal. 5:22-23) showing us that the all surpassing power of Him who is in us, is truly greater than he who is in the world. (1 John 4:4)

John 4:6-7 indicates a Samaritan woman came to Jacob's well. Jacob's well "was not a spring-fed well, but a well into which water seeped from rain and dew, collecting at the bottom."[viii] In contrast what type of water did Jesus offer her (verse 10)?

_____

Fresh and pure living water! A water that could quench spiritual thirst forever!

Side note: what does John 4:6 record as Jesus' physical state?

_____

Tired!

If we fill up with the Living Water of His Word first thing in the morning, we will have enough to pour out throughout our day even in worn out exhaustion to accomplish HIS agenda and to-do list for us each day. How willing are you to seek out a filling of His Living Water daily? How willing are you to take up His list, His agenda and lay down yours?

_____

_____

How do you practically "fill up" day to day? Anything filling us other than our Creator God will eventually run dry, come up short, leaving us dehydrated, unsatisfied and empty. What happens to a car engine when you try to run it without oil or you put the wrong gas type into the tank?! Such it will be with a soul void of Jesus. Are there things that you may need to exchange or change in order to have room for the right fill up?

_____

_____

John 4:11-12 records the woman's many concerns and questions however it seems her focus and concern are on the wrong thing? She expresses concern over Jesus' lack of rope or bucket, and does He know just how deep the well really is?! I wonder if we have ever sounded similar in our prayers with Him.

His response in verse 13 and 14 contrasts the world's water with His water. If our focus remained on our Source rather than our lack of resources, we might be able to lay aside many of our worries and fears. The Source is never lacking more resources. Is there anything in your life that you need to shift your focus from the resource to The Source?

_____

John 4:25 (NLT) gives us what this woman does know, *The woman said, "I know the Messiah is coming-the one who is called Christ. When he comes, he will explain everything to us."*

Dear one, in all that we do not understand now, let us not misunderstand that one day we will not regret sticking with Him by faith in His trustworthy Word. Ecclesiastes 3:11 (NLT) assures us, *Yet as God has made everything beautiful for its own time. He has planted eternity in the human heart, but even so, people cannot see the whole scope of God's work from beginning to end.*

In John 4:15 she expresses her desire for this Living Water. Why?

_____

So she won't have to come and draw water anymore and probably not have to continue to dodge the judgmental stares of the other women at the well due to her life style depicted in verses 17-18. Once she does receive the Truth of Jesus what does she do (verse 29)?

_____

She surrounds herself with others, exclaiming what she knows about Him, unashamed!! When we get Jesus, we do not want to hide away we want to share His abounding goodness, His redeeming grace with everyone (Jeremiah 20:9)!

Despite her shady past, what does Jesus choose to reveal to this woman, this outcast, this sinful Samaritan as society would call her (see verse 26)?

_____

He reveals to her that He is I AM. He is the long-awaited Messiah! In her questions all throughout this passage whether it was with correct focus or not or to get Him to stop probing at her lifestyle or whether it was regarding the proper place of worship... maybe in all the dialog Jesus sensed her thirst to know Him truly and without making her fix herself first, He freely gave of Himself (even in exhaustion). He gave and she transformed within, not the other way around.

Unlike Nicodemus in John 3 this woman humbly received and then in humility gave (as per Jesus' example toward her) and an entire village was transformed! Who is in your "village" your sphere of influence?

_____

(Do not worry this is not the end of Nicodemus' story.)

In John 4:27 the disciples come back with questions they decide not even to ask. I wonder if at this moment they had come to just expect the unexpected with Jesus or if they had been wondering why Jesus had allowed THEM to even stick around and follow Him! It may have become a bit clearer in that moment that as He wanted them, He wanted her, He wanted/wants EVERYONE.

Do you know you are wanted?
You are wanted.

What question is asked in John 4:33?

_____

What is Jesus' response in the very next verse?

_____

Our nourishment, our purpose is to fulfill His will. What is His will? To plant the good seed of His Word into hearts, to encourage those seeds to grow into a lifesaving knowledge of Jesus Christ, to be a part of the work that is to increase the harvest for His Kingdom. This does not mean you have to travel around the world… maybe it does, but maybe it is serving in the nursery so that a young mom can attend the church service. Be the vessel for His love right where you are at with what you have and let Him grow the harvest, as only He can do. (1 Cor. 3:7)

Please turn to Luke 4:14-15 and we see that Jesus has arrived where now?

_____

Galilee. Jesus made it to his destination, but He did not waste the journey.

Let us not waste our journey.

Thank you muchly dear one, I pray you felt our journey in His Word today was well worth the time and effort as much as I did. Please record what impacted your heart the deepest before signing off for today.

_____

_____

_____

_____

Day 6 & 7: At His Feet – A Time to Reflect

Over the next two days take time to reflect over your week of study. Maybe you need some time to catch up on the study material and this might be the perfect break to do just that with the Lord!

I encourage you to glance back at the final point at the end of each day that you recorded having had the greatest impact on your heart. As you spend time with God in prayer, reflect and record on the lines below how God is tying it together and applying it to your life specifically for such a time as this.

Ask that God make it clear who He would have you invite into an opportunity to share Him, to apply what you are learning; maybe a child, grandchild, friend… trust Him to continue to take the lead. May we have a heart ever ready with eyes and ears out to the opportunities God wants to invite us into for His glory and praise.

Do not merely listen to the word, and so deceive yourselves. Do what it says. Anyone who listens to the word but does not do what it says is like someone who looks at his face in a mirror and, after looking at himself, goes away and immediately forgets what he looks like. But whoever looks intently into the perfect law that gives freedom, and continues in it – not forgetting what they have heard, but doing it – they will be blessed in what they do. James 1:22-25 (NIV)

_____

_____

_____

_____

_____

_____

_____

_____

_____

_____

Philippians 4:13 (NIV) *I can do all this through him who gives me strength.*

John 14:26 (NIV) *But the Advocate, the Holy Spirit, whom the Father will send in my name, will teach you all things and will remind you of everything I have said to you.*

WEEK 6

For since the creation of the world God's invisible qualities – his eternal power and divine nature – have been clearly seen, being understood from what has been made, so that people are without excuse. Romans 1:20 (NIV)

Day 1: EXTAordinary

Welcome, I am so glad you are here. You are extraordinary for sure! The level of effort you have poured forth to have made it thus far in this study is exceptional. I know God will honor your faithful diligence to prioritize spending quality time with Him. May we press on in all the strength and energy Christ so powerfully and faithfully provides (Colossians 1:29).

Please begin in prayer and then head back to John 4 where we left off last week. Read John 4:43-54. _____

This is the second miracle Jesus did in Cana. What was the first (verse 46)?

_____

Whose son gets miraculously healed in this passage?

_____

"The official was probably a Gentile centurion, possibly in the service of Herod Antipas (cf. Mark 6:14). John shows Jesus bringing the gospel to a respected Jewish teacher (John 3:1-21), then to an outcast Samaritan woman (4:1-42), then to an official working for the Roman government (4:46-54), and thus, by implication from these examples, to everyone in the world."[ix]

Jesus has come for EVERYONE which was His plan from the very beginning.

The world at that time did not quite understand His mission and still today it often goes misinterpreted. Jesus came for all; it is up to us to choose Him back. Our choosing will impact the way we live and where we live eternally.

Is how we live for Him creating a contrast to the ways of the world? Jesus knew how to stand out in a way that invited people into Himself. He invites all and with acceptance of Him we invite life change that will create a contrast the world will take notice of.

Record some ways you stand out in your sphere of influence? What contrast, in His love, do you bring to this world so that others might see a magnification of Jesus?

_____

Do not fear if the contrast you create in this world is not always well received. Please read Luke 4:16-30. _____

Can you just imagine all the jaws in the room dropping at verse 21?! Wild right!?!!

Luke 4:22 records the questions of the people, what are they?

Are we willing to give the unexpected a chance, or will we miss out on the extraordinary because it is hidden in the ordinary?

Read from the Old Testament the Scriptures Jesus read in the synagogue that Sabbath day. See Isaiah 61:1-2 and continue through verse 3. _____

This is a picture of contrast. These verses do not depict the way of the world but rather the way of Jesus. Have you accepted Jesus within you? Do you feel rich with Good News? Have you received His comfort over a broken heart? Have you been a prisoner set free? Do you feel the Lord's favor through the forgiveness of sin? Have you been rebuilt into beauty from ash? Do you have the joy of the Lord rather than hopeless despair? If yes on any account then you have experienced the contrast of Christ... now dear one, go be His EXTAordinary vessel.

But thanks be to God, who in Christ always leads us in triumphal procession, and through us spreads the fragrance of the knowledge of him everywhere. 2 Corinthians 2:14 (ESV) Please record the nugget of greatest impact for you today below. Thank you!

_____
_____
_____
_____

Day 2: Who Is in Your Boat?

Hello (insert friendly smile). I just finished mixing up some Kool-Aid for my kids. Have you ever had a sip of Kool-Aid that has not been stirred well? It is horrible! The Kool-Aid packet along with the sugar must be thoroughly mixed and stirred up so that the elements permeate entirely. If the mix just sits settled at the bottom of the pitcher the result is only worthy of being spit out. Such it is with our spiritual life I believe (Rev. 3:16). Unless a healthy dose of holy reverential fear is stirred up within our soul our spiritual life is flat out bland. If we are not careful, we may have been drinking unstirred Kool-Aid for so long that it seems acceptable! I am praying we settle for nothing short of allowing His Spirit to be thoroughly stirred up in us today!

The fear of the LORD is the beginning of wisdom, and knowledge of the Holy One is understanding. Proverbs 9:10 (NIV) Let's use this verse as a stir stick and pray God begin to stir up His Spirit within us to create such a tidal wave of reverential holy fear for the Author of all authority that we'll get swept to thrilling heights in Him we never could have fathomed on our own!

Let's go fishin'! I hope you brought your rod for all the good things I already sense we are going to catch in our hearts today! Please turn and read this account from three different perspectives.

Matthew 4:18-22 _____
Mark 1:16-20 _____
Luke 5:1-11 _____

The passage that records the most detail of this event, Luke 5:2 tells us how many boats were at the water's edge?

_____

Two. Jesus steps into one and asks the owner (Peter) if He can use it. Jesus offers us all an invitation to be involved in what He is doing. Peter could have said, "no" and Jesus could have moved on to the second boat. Good golly if Jesus sees a use for my "boat" I want it to be available to Him!

Yes, there can be fear involved… looking at this story Peter had not met with much success that night before and yet God was asking the guy with a boat full of empty failure to push out DEEPER and try again!!! I heard once that courage is just fear that has said its prayers and that what we would look at and call an empty boat of failure, to God is just a boat with a whole lot of room for His redeeming grace!

Does your boat have room for Him?! Sometimes our success can cause us to forget that really, we can do nothing apart from Him. Might we make sure that with each success He brings into our "boat" we continually get on our face like Peter does in verse 8. Allowing awestruck wonder, a healthy dose of holy fear to be stirred up within us at just Who has brought about such success! In humility thank Him for using our "boat".

Really who's boat is it anyway? Who grew the tree that the wood came from to build it? Who created the brain with the ability to design the boat? Who gave you the means to acquire such a vessel? In His grace He gave us each a boat and by His grace He offers us an opportunity to give it back. What do you have as a "boat"? What do you have in your "boat" that God might want to use for His glory? Has He called you to courageously go out deeper with Him?

_____

_____

_____

In Luke 5:7 who is called over to help with the load?

_____

When God blesses us with a blessing it is never just for us. Who might be in the water near you that might share in a blessing God has given you?

_____

_____

Luke 5:10 records Jesus telling the boys not to be afraid, now they would fish for people. This verse records them leaving everything to follow Him! There was no recorded complaining, worrying or hesitation. They did not worry that they had not gone to "fish for people" school! Why?! In both the way Matthew 4:19 and Mark 1:17 record this incident in the NLT, Jesus relays that if they will follow Him, He will SHOW them how to fish for people!

Dear one, do you feel unqualified for what He has called you to?! He has given you His Word and as Jesus followed the Word while on earth and made time to always pray, His example proves He was always well equipped!

Read Hebrews 4:12, 2 Timothy 3:16-17.

He will always provide for His purpose, cast yourself onto Him and trust that He will always be enough. Pray for courage and as you step into the situation, He leads you to, you will find He is already there with all the courage you need to stand.

A butterfly never went to cocoon making school either. That caterpillar must rely on God for every placement of silk only to find himself stuck in a tight restrictive tube!!! I am sure he has his doubts that he has done things right and from all enclosed angles he probably feels ineffective! However, in patient trusting endurance the miraculous happens and he emerges transformed! God knew what he was doing with that caterpillar's life all along, that little guy needed to trust, listen and obey.

Do you have a situation in which you are in or have been in that relates to this butterfly analogy?

_____
_____
_____

We must trust His process in the cocoon if we are ever going to emerge as the butterfly He planned dear one. Please record how God impacted you the most while in His Word today.

_____
_____
_____
_____

Day 3: Ultimate Authority

That miracle we studied yesterday with fish was fantastic! Are you ready to be dazed at this demolition of demons?! Before we jump into our adventure today please begin in prayer acknowledging that God Almighty, our ultimate authority, must lead.

Please read Mark 1:21-28. _____
Please read Luke 4:31-37. _____

As this story begins what is it that amazes these people about Jesus' teaching in the synagogue?

_____

The authority by which He spoke! It is much different when an author speaks about their work compared to someone who has just done research on another's work. Jesus is the Author of all Scripture; can you imagine hearing Him explain and teach it?! WOW!

The questions in this passage are posed by an evil spirit. What do the questions indicate to us?

_____

The demons know who He is and His authority over them is made clear in this passage. Even the spiritual underworld was aware that Jesus was the Messiah.

James 2:19 (NIV) states, *You believe that there is one God. Good! Even the demons believe that--and shudder.*

Do we tremble at His name? In holy fear do we reverence just Who our finite minds will never fully comprehend? Do we embrace the Truth with faces pressed to the floor that as Majestic as He is, He chooses to love us with a love that exceeds our comprehension? (Psalm 8:3-4)

We have looked at His authority over nature such as the fish in the sea yet He humbly asks to involve our "boats"; we have seen His authority over, and acknowledged by, even the spiritual underworld... let's look at His power over illness coupled with a compassion for the ill one.

Please read Matthew 8:14-17 _____, Mark 1:29-34 _____ and Luke 4:38-41. _____

I enjoy Matthew's gospel as it continues to point out Jesus' fulfillment of the Old Testament. Matthew 8:17 points us to Jesus fulfilling Isaiah 53:4.

Please take a moment to read Isaiah 53. _____
This chapter is an astounding prophecy of Jesus' sacrifice on the cross for us. Who would have thought God would save the world in such a humble way! God's way and plan was/is so contrary to the prideful way of humanity.

Often God's ways differ from our own (Isaiah 55:8-9). Ultimate strength is displayed in gentleness, humility and merciful submission. How hard is it for you to withhold strength when it is in your power to unleash it? When you can hold your tongue, forgive first, surrender or sacrifice your will for the good of another especially when the other has not been good to you... that is a display of ultimate strength - strength under control is a quality that magnifies the character of Christ.

In Luke 4:38-41 the scenario is recorded as though everyone was asking (the NLT uses the word, *begging*) Jesus to heal Peter's mother in law. She must have been someone many admired and looked up to. What are some remarkable qualities that you find admirable in another?

_____

_____

Do you know someone like you have just described? Have you encouraged them lately by telling them the specifics about them that encourage you?

_____

Matthew and Mark both tell us that Jesus did what, to heal this woman?

_____

He reached out and touched her hand. He had to come in close to do that. He is close to the broken hearted (Psalm 34:18). We can pray regularly for a heightened sense of Him. Matthew 13:16 (NIV) states, *But blessed are your eyes because they see, and your ears because they hear.*

What does this MIL do as soon as she is healed?

_____

She begins to serve!! How are we using the gift of our moment? My brother said once that he lays in bed just a minute longer in the mornings just to wiggle his fingers and toes and say, "Thanks God".

Is there anything you have been taking for granted that might be used to serve Him back in this gift of a moment you have been given?

_____

_____

As the sun went down Jesus continued to work and Luke records, by the touch of His hand He was healing everyone! Again, our attention is drawn to the compassion God Almighty has on His creation.

Luke 4:41 relates to us that again Jesus will not let the demons speak. Jesus was on mission and would not allow the enemy a word in edgewise to distract or detour His purpose. How might we follow suit and intentionally infiltrate our hearts and minds with His Truth and block the enemies lies as we walk out His mission for our lives?

_____

_____

And let us consider how we may spur one another on toward love and good deeds, not giving up meeting together, as some are in the habit of doing, but encouraging one another - and all the more as you see the Day approaching. Hebrews 10:24-25 (NIV)

You have been a source of encouragement to me. Thank you. *'May the LORD bless you and protect you. May the LORD smile on you and be gracious to you. May the LORD show you his favor and give you his peace.'* Numbers 6:24-26 (NLT)

Let us break here for today. Please record the encouragement God Himself has brought to your heart.

_____

_____

_____

_____

Day 4: Stop, Drop & PRAY

Hello dearly beloved of God. Thank you for your diligence in pursuing excellence in the study of your God. I pray as you meet with Him today that you receive an overflowing dose of joy, peace and hope as the Holy Spirit stirs up within you all that you have allowed to fall into your heart from His Truth. Pray to follow His lead.

Please read Matthew 4:23-25 _____, Mark 1:35-39 _____ and Luke 4:42-44. _____

Mark and Luke record the source of Jesus' strength to face the masses and to stay on course with why He was sent. What was it and when do each of these passages record when He did it?

_____

Prayer. BEFORE the day began.

Please record the following verses below.

Psalm 5:3

_____

_____

Psalm 143:8

_____

_____

Do you remember as a kid practicing your fire escape route in your home? Or do you remember the stop, drop and roll drill in school that was always so fun to practice because it always ended in a pile of laughter on the floor as everyone rolled all over the place?!! All funny business aside "stop, drop and roll" can save your life if you ever found yourself on fire.

I think this can be applied to our spiritual life. Instead of "stop, drop and roll" think, "stop, drop and pray". In any situation, but especially "fiery" ones this action could save your life.

He has begun a good work in each one of us that He promises to finish (Phil. 1:6). He knows our way and has just specifically what we will need to face everything fully equipped; a tailored Word just for us. Why would we be too busy to receive it? It is like jumping ship without a life preserver!

Just as Jesus sat beside the well in Samaria waiting for that dear woman, don't you know He waits for you, for me too?! How often do we leave Him waiting in our early hours only to cry out to Him later in the day as an ill equipped hot mess, half drowned from trying to swim the ocean of our day all on our own?!

Does it stir a revenant holy fear in anyone else that in spite of the hot mess I so often become, the God of the universe, the God who breathed galaxies into the sky yet intricately builds the delicately detailed butterfly's wing as it waits trusting His hand... says to me even still, "Dear one, I'm enthralled by your beauty (Psalm 45:11), take My hand, I am here, I will help you."

For I am the LORD you God who takes hold of your right hand and says to you, Do not fear; I will help you. Isaiah 41:13 (NIV)

I pray He has stirred up your heart as He has mine to a craving so deep for more of Him that it will not be satisfied but by ever increasing amounts of Him!

As you praise Him please record that which He has impacted your heart with most today during your study.

_____

_____

_____

_____

Day 5: Be a vessel… of Live Hope

"Comin' in hot!!" Hello my friend. This exclamation is something our adventure seeking youngest child will yell at the top of his lungs as he rides his bike in at full speed like he's flying a jet plane in to land somewhere on the launch pad (otherwise known as our driveway)! This child experiences life to its fullest, there is no room for the word "fear" in his vocabulary, only opportunity for "thrill"! In Jesus we can live life on the live wire of hope too. Today I am praying Romans 15:13 would become a reality for us and that in our… comin' and goin's… we would be doin' it hot, alive with Living Hope!

Romans 15:13 (NIV) *May the God of hope fill you with all joy and peace as you trust in him, so that you may overflow with hope by the power of the Holy Spirit.*

Please read John 5:1-15. _____

What question does Jesus ask in verse 6?

_____

"Do you want to get well?" (NIV) I almost hear Him asking, "Can I heal your will?"

What is the response of the man who had been lying there ill for 38 years?!

_____

I can't… I have no one to help… someone always gets ahead of me… Any of these experiences, especially over a period of 38 years is enough to kill a will.

The attitude of "I can't…" is a stumbling block before the race even begins. Secondly, we cannot blame others for not fulfilling in us what only Jesus can. The blame game and the comparison game are also sure to backfire. Our faith hope and focus should be grounded in His validation of us and of Who He is in His Word.

Have you been where you felt you lost your will to try? Maybe for a season or a moment or just within a certain circumstance or situation? Can you put a finger on why you felt this way?

I like the saying; the only disability is a bad attitude. With the right attitude there will always be hope from a living angle. Jesus is our Living Hope and in Him it is not a glass half full or half empty it is a glass we each get as a gift and in Him it is refillable!

Peter 1:3 (NIV) *Praise be to the God and Father of our Lord Jesus Christ! In his great mercy he has given us new birth into a living hope though the resurrection of Jesus Christ from the dead,*

In our John 5 passage this gentleman when asked by Jesus if he wanted to get well, did not even consider it a possibility. After 38 years he had given up hope. Can we blame him?! However, he was still hanging out near the pool in which some believed there could be healing.

This 38-year-old man answered Jesus' question with, "I can't…" maybe he still believed for others just not himself. But see Jesus did not make it an issue of can or can't, He made it a question of want. Jesus does heal this man's legs but maybe it was to prove that He was God and a God that still believed at 38 this man could walk free of guilt and shame and could live eternally.

It was not and isn't a question of *can* Jesus forgive you, but rather will you trust Him to do so? Do you believe He can restore others but just not you? Do you feel you're too far gone; you've failed too many times? Dear one, beloved of God Almighty, that is just not so!!! Unfailing redeeming grace is His professional business!

He will not force Himself on any of us, true love is not forced, but will you let Him love you (He already does) but will you allow Him to stir your soul to a living breathing life made new in Him, walking set free, completely free!?!! Do you want to get well? Let Him heal your will to live walking truly set free.

Where did Jesus find this man who had been healed in John 5:14?

_____

I believe this man was in a state of awestruck worship. Jesus finds him at the temple and gives him what advice (verse 14)?

_____

The man is well and has been fully restored! Jesus warns him now to make a change, stop sinning. We too are to be intentional in guarding our freedom, our victory in Christ! Once we have been freed, we need to pivot toward God make no allowances for anything at any cost to come between you and God. Often, it is the small things that are more dangerous than the big things in getting their hooks back into a freed individual. It is often a slow fade yet a slippery slope.
Please read 2 Timothy 1:14, Matthew 12:43-45, 1 Peter 5:8.

And what did this healed man do in verse 15?

_____

When you have been set free your heart will sing His praise in worship and the hope will be uncontainable just as it was for the woman at the well! Psalm 107:2 (NIV) *Let the redeemed of the LORD tell their story-- those he redeemed from the hand of the foe,*

Do you have a story you would like to share below as you sing His praises?
_____

Let us end today on that high note of praise shall we! Please record what made the biggest impact to your heart today while you studied. See you soon!
_____
_____
_____
_____

Day 6 & 7: At His Feet – A Time to Reflect

Over the next two days take time to reflect over your week of study. Maybe you need some time to catch up on the study material and this might be the perfect break to do just that with the Lord!

I encourage you to glance back at the final point at the end of each day that you recorded having had the greatest impact on your heart. As you spend time with God in prayer, reflect and record on the lines below how God is tying it together and applying it to your life specifically for such a time as this.

Ask that God make it clear who He would have you invite into an opportunity to share Him, to apply what you are learning; maybe a child, grandchild, friend… trust Him to continue to take the lead. May we have a heart ever ready with eyes and ears out to the opportunities God wants to invite us into for His glory and praise.

Do not merely listen to the word, and so deceive yourselves. Do what it says. Anyone who listens to the word but does not do what it says is like someone who looks at his face in a mirror and, after looking at himself, goes away and immediately forgets what he looks like. But whoever looks intently into the perfect law that gives freedom, and continues in it – not forgetting what they have heard, but doing it – they will be blessed in what they do.
James 1:22-25 (NIV)

_____
_____
_____
_____
_____
_____
_____
_____
_____

Philippians 4:13 (NIV) *I can do all this through him who gives me strength.*

John 14:26 (NIV) *But the Advocate, the Holy Spirit, whom the Father will send in my name, will teach you all things and will remind you of everything I have said to you.*

WEEK 7

See, I am doing a new thing a new thing! Now it springs up; do you not perceive it? I am making a way in the wilderness and streams in the wasteland. Isaiah 43:19 (NIV)

Day 1: Hope-FULL Faith

And hope does not put us to shame, because God's love has been poured out into our hearts through the Holy Spirit, who has been given to us. Romans 5:5 (NIV) On that firm and trustworthy note let's bend our knee and acknowledge the Source of our unfailing hope.

Today's hope filled Word will be found in Matthew 8:1-4 ____, Mark 1:40-45____ and Luke 5:12-16. ____

A side note…

Matthew's gospel is considered the Jewish Gospel and often points out how the Torah was fulfilled in Jesus. Mark centers on Jesus as Messiah and Son of God along with the nature of true discipleship. Luke has more of a social concern highlighting the importance of prayer, the Spirit and worship. (*NLT Parallel Study Bible* notes, pg. 1721) "In John, Jesus is the living revealer of God who encounters all people with the 'light of the world' and the 'bread of life' and with the need to believe."[x]

Just as it's beneficial to look through the lens of the different vantage points God has provided in the four gospels in order to gain a clearer picture of Who He is, He has also placed a different angle of the jewel through which to see Him more clearly in the world within each of us!

You are a vessel reflecting a fresh angle of Him to the world through your personal experiences and walk with Him. The jewel He has placed in you will reflect His Light at just the right angle for someone else to see Him more clearly than they ever have before! Keep shining (Matthew 5:16)!

Okay. In the passages listed above that we just read in Matthew, Mark and Luke; we saw Jesus healing what deadly disease?

_____

People with Leprosy were considered unclean outcasts. It was a feared, highly contagious disease of which there was no known cure.

Our passage in Luke (NLT) tells us in verse 5:12 that this man had an advanced case. In each of the three passages it is recorded that this man asked Jesus if He was *willing* to heal him… this man did not ask if Jesus was *able* which indicates a spark of hopeful faith that maybe, just maybe he could be healed.

Verse 41 in Mark's gospel chapter 1 (NLT) indicates Jesus was moved with compassion. How is this man healed in contrast to the lame man we just read about in John 5 on day five last week?

_____

The lame man was healed by just a word. So even though we know Jesus could have healed with a word he was moved with such compassion toward this "untouchable", highly contagious man and chooses to heal him with a TOUCH!

Please read Revelation 21:4 and record what His touch will do for each one of us in the end or rather our real beginning in Christ?

_____

_____

Luke 5:15-16 tells us Jesus' fame was spreading like wildfire however what continued to ground Jesus to His main purpose (verse 16)?

_____

No matter what swirled around Him, good or bad, He remained constant in His wholehearted devotion to His relationship with the Father. OFTEN Jesus withdrew to the wilderness to pray.

How often do you find time to withdraw and pray, to nurture your relationship with your Heavenly Father?

_____

As a mother of six I understand the way you "withdraw to the wilderness and pray" (as it is stated similarly in the NLT) looks different as the seasons of life change. If you keep Him priority during constant change, He will give you the constant creativity to remain consistently steadfast in a nurturing relationship with Him. There will always be just enough energy and strength to again go to Him for more.

We have seen our God is a God that can heal with His word, He can heal with His touch. He is a God who is moved by compassion and is willing to heal our will to do so. Not all healing comes this side of heaven like we would like. This world is broken in sin, but Jesus has made a way out for all who choose to believe! All sin can be wiped clean this side of heaven so that we can make it to the other side in which we will experience complete and total healing. That is faith FULL of hope dear one!

Please enjoy 2 Corinthians 5:1-10 in closing today. _____

Please record how God impacted your heart the most today and I will see you back here tomorrow. I am already looking forward to it in hope-FULL expectation!

_____
_____
_____
_____

Day 2: The Stir Stick of Fear

Welcome back dear one. Thank you for meeting me here as we near the middle of your week when often the pressures of life are at their highest. It is from that middle ground we often find ourselves looking out in all directions with increasing discouragement. In the middle we are too far from our destination to see it clearly and too far from where we came from to justify heading back. I pray that right in the middle ground of this week, and of each of your moments, you are able to grab that stick of discouragement or fear that the enemy hands you and use it to stir up a healthy dose of devil defeating praise that you still have a middle!!! Middle's really do make the best launch pads so may we launch right into the middle of the life reviving sea of His Word!!

Proceed after prayer please.

Read:
Matthew 9:1-8 _____
Mark 2:1-12 _____
Luke 5:17-26. _____

Each passage tells us Jesus sees what?

_____

He sees their faith! How does one "see" faith (see James 2:17)?

_____

Works do not earn faith, but faith is proved genuine by works. A healthy apple tree will naturally produce fruit if its branches remains connected to the tree. Remain connected to Jesus and your life will naturally prove your faith genuine.

In what ways have you had an opportunity to see your faith prove genuine?

_____
_____

Jesus saw the great effort these men were going to, to bring their friend to Him. They proved they believed Jesus could heal if only they could get to Him. Jesus saw their faith. He was also able to read the hearts of the judgmental Pharisees and calls them out on their doubt. What is the question in the hearts of the Pharisees?

_____
They questioned His claim to God.
How does Jesus respond to this? Record Jesus' statement in Matthew 9:6 below.

_____
The Son of Man has authority on earth.

Let us look at this title, "Son of Man". Jesus is claiming to be the One depicted in Daniel 7:13-14 NKJV, *"I was watching in the night visions, And behold, One like the Son of Man, Coming with the clouds of heaven! He came to the Ancient of Days, And they brought Him near before Him. Then to Him was given dominion and glory and a kingdom, That all peoples, nations, and languages should serve Him. His dominion is an everlasting dominion, Which shall not pass away, And His kingdom the one Which shall not be destroyed.*

Matthew 3:17 makes it clear that Jesus is God's Son. Jesus referring to Himself as the Son of Man builds a bridge, a way to connect mankind to the Father.

Matthew 9:8 (NLT) states that after Jesus healed this man's sins and physically healed his paralysis, Fear swept through the crowd as they saw this happen. And they praised God for sending a man with such great authority.

A fear that stirred up praise! Oh, that we might trust Him enough to allow all that creates fear within us to be what triggers a response of mighty praise!

Mark 2:12 (NIV) ends with, *"We've never seen anything like this before!"* 1 Cor. 2:9 tells us in a sense, what God has prepared for those who persevere in their love for Him will blow our minds! We will have never seen anything of the sort! Praise Him!

The Son of God, the Son of Man, the Author of authority maintains control, He governs with compassion and His heart is willing and moved on our behalf to increase the faith of the willing to be moved. Who are we that He is mindful of us?! (Psalm 8:3-4)

Before we close today please glance at three more segments of Scripture that verify His willing heart, His arm that is not too short to save nor that His ear is too dull to hear. (Isaiah 59:1)

Please read Matthew 9:9-13 _____, Mark 2:13-17 _____, Luke 5:27-32 _____.
Levi is Matthew just to clarify. We see in each of these passages Jesus is on the way, He is on the move and His eyes are out. How often do you think you have been on your way out the door or on the road and have failed to see God's divine appointment because it was disguised as a distraction or an interruption?

The Pharisees again question Jesus' actions because Matthew was a tax collector and despised by many as they were often dishonest people. The passage in Luke chapter 5 verse 30 (NLT) records the Pharisees complaining bitterly! When you are constantly with a judgmental attitude often it stems from bitterness does it not!?! The bitterness of jealousy, or unforgiveness, or any number of other insecurities and hurts can eat away at us if not given over to God for His healing touch.

What is Jesus' response to these bitter complaints (see Luke 5:31)?

_____

In Matthew 9:13 Jesus uses their question again as an opportunity to point to the Scriptures! When we have questions look to the Scriptures for our answer. Jesus in this instance says, I want you to show mercy, not offer sacrifices. Please look up Hosea 6:6 and Micah 6:6-8 and record what God places value on from us.

_____

In each of these passages, Jesus is contrasting what?

_____

Thinking vs. knowing. Thinking you are good versus knowing you are a sinner and need a Savior makes all the difference in the world. How do you think recognizing your need for Him in all things effects how He is able to use you effectively?

_____

_____

After Jesus invites the uninvited how does humble gratitude reveal this man's faith in Matt. 9:10?

_____

Matthew (or Levi) invites Him back! Jesus is welcomed into his home where, like the Samaritan woman, Levi exposes his whole "village" to Jesus! How has your acceptance of Jesus' invitation to believe, to accept His redeeming grace, to join Him in His work, given you an opportunity to return the invite? How have you invited Him back into your "village"?

_____

_____

Taking a moment to remember what we have studied recently...

- Our God the Author of all authority, the Creator of all life is moved by a heart of compassion toward His creation. He longs to heal our deteriorating bodies from the effects of a broken and sinful world; and one day we will all be made whole.

- He is a God who cares to heal even our will and to forgive our sin! He is the Son of Man who has bridged the gap to the Father by way of the cross, sacrificing His own life in place of our own.

- By a word He brings healing and through His touch we are transformed, in His love we are redeemed!

- May fear be only a stick that stirs up monumental praise within us.

- We may not see all things done in our way and in our time but in His best time and in His best way, He's "comin' in hot" for us (as my son would say)! His return will be like nothing we have ever seen and then all things will be made new! Let that truth stir up some holy fear and authentic praise!

Before we close please read Revelation 19:11-16 as you allow the magnitude of this Truth to stir up within you a holy reverential fear of just Who He is; Live Hope! Praise the one whose name is Faithful and True! Now go be a vessel alive with Living Hope for His glory!

Please indicate below the thing that made the most impact on your heart today. Thank you muchly~

_____
_____
_____
_____

Day 3: Be a vessel… Of the Son of God

Welcome friend. Thank you again for walking this path with me. Psalm 23:4 (ESV) starts, *Even though I walk through the valley of the shadow.* Shadows can be scary, but you know a shadow is only evidence that there is light somewhere and, in a light, we can read His Word which Psalm 119:105 (NIV) verifies for us. *Your word is a lamp for my feet, a light on my path.* Praying He light our way today.

One for our hearts pocket: *For with you is the fountain of life; in your light we see light.* Psalm 36:9 (NIV)

Let's join a discussion we can see recorded in three spots, Matthew 9:14-17 _____, Mark 2:18-22 _____, and Luke 5:33-39. _____

Each passage depicts the same question of Jesus that stems from comparison. Basically, some people approach Jesus asking why do the followers of John the Baptist and the Pharisees fast and pray regularly but Yours eat and drink?!

Think about it… how much of worry and anxiety stems from some angle of comparison or another?!

When we too start looking around at other people for validation on who we are and what we are doing we end up in a pile of over-thought confusion! At least we see these people going to the source to gain clarification rather than spread their own speculations. Do you tend to go to the source when you have a question, or do you fester in your own speculations?

_____

Jesus is always open for the asking. He was patient with these people, and He is patient with our questions too. Just as He used this question as an opportunity to try and offer them more of who He wanted to be to them I too think He sees our questions as opportunities to bring to light more of Who He wants to be to us.

Like John the Baptist used the illustration of a wedding regarding the relationship to the Messiah (John 3:29) which draws on Old Testament writings (see Isaiah 54:5-6) Jesus now also uses that illustration. The church is considered the bride of Christ which illustrates the kind of relationship He desires with us.

Going from Luke 5:36-38 what two illustrations does Jesus give them?

_____

_____

"New cloth shrinks when washed and so tears the old; new wine expands with fermentation and breaks brittle old wineskins. In either case, both old and new are ruined. Both illustrations make the point that the old is incompatible with the new. Jesus did not come to patch up the old covenant, but to establish a new one. The Kingdom of God brings a whole new orientation to thinking and living."[xi]

Read Hebrews 12:18-29 to see contrast between the two covenants. _____

Change is hard for many even if it is for the better and as you can see in Luke 5:39 it was in that day too. How open are you to new people, ideas, programs? Can you think of an example in your life that required you to go through change... how did it go? What did you learn?

_____

_____

Fill in the blanks below according to Ezekiel 36:26 (NIV).

I will give you a _____ _____ and put a _____ _____ in you; I will remove from you your _____ ____ _____ and give you a heart of _____.

(new heart, new spirit, heart of stone, flesh)

How willing are you to let God do heart surgery on you? Have you ever witnessed a heart transformation in someone or even yourself? You may even have had several hypothetical heart transplants throughout your life if you are as old as I! Take a moment to reflect on this thought as we close.

I'm praying to be open to heart surgery whenever the Great Physician sees need of it; laying an open heart in the skilled and trustworthy hands of our Heavenly Father who knit it together in the first place guarantees there will always be room for Him. That equals an eternal survival rate every time.
Please record the greatest impact from today's study below.

_____

_____

_____

_____

Day 4: Choose Life

Welcome back! Let us jump right on in without delay but first… pray. Pray for a prepared heart to receive a tailored Word. Nothing like the presence of the God in a heart to revive life!

Please read John 5:16-47. _____

In this passage Jesus clearly claims to be equal with God the Father as God's Son.

1 John 5:11 (NLT) is one to tuck in our hearts pocket. *And this is what God has testified: He has given us eternal life, and this life is in his Son.*

"The Old Testament mentioned three signs of the coming Messiah. In this chapter, John shows that Jesus has fulfilled all three signs. Authority to judge is given to him as the Son of Man (compare 5:27 with Dan. 7:13-14). The lame and sick are healed (compare 5:20-21 with Isa. 35:6; Jer. 31:8-9). The dead are raised to life (compare 5:21, 28 with Deut. 32:39; 1 Sam. 2:6; 2 Kings 5:7)."[xii]

In Jesus' testimony He provides multiple witnesses in this passage. God's law requires more than one witness (Deut. 17:6) so He begins with God Himself (Jn. 5:32), remember Mark 1:11 the Father's voice declared it at His baptism. Then John the Baptist (Jn. 5:33) himself pointed to Jesus as the Messiah (John 1:29-34). Thirdly there were all the miraculous signs and wonders that He did (Jn. 5:36) more evidence pointing to Who His Father was and thus Who He Was! Then there are the Scriptures themselves (Jn. 5:39)! Luke 24:25-27 clearly states the Scriptures point to the Messiah and that Jesus was the fulfillment! (*NLT Study Bible* notes, pg. 1988)

Deut. 30:19-20 (NLT) *"Today I have given you the choice between life and death, between blessings and curses. Now I call on heaven and earth to witness the choice you make. Oh, that you would choose life, so that you and your descendants might life! You can make this choice by loving the LORD your God, obeying him, and committing yourself firmly to him. This is the key to your life....*

John 14:6 (NIV) *Jesus answered, "I am the way and the truth and the life. No one comes to the Father except through me.*

Please savor 1 Corinthians 6:9-11 (NLT) below.

(9-10) *Don't you realize that those who do wrong will not inherit the Kingdom of God? Don't fool yourselves. Those who indulge in sexual sin, or who worship idols, or commit adultery, or are male prostitutes, or practice homosexuality, or are thieves, or greedy people, or drunkards, or are abusive, or cheat people-none of these will inherit the Kingdom of God.*

Who among us could make it in?! Worship idols... maybe we did not carve one out of the front yard tree and bow to it but have any of us turned a loved one or a career into an idol of sorts?! Anyone?! We are all guilty on some count or another! But praise Him there is another verse!! (See 1 Corinthians 6:11 (NLT) below.)

(11) *Some of you were once like that. But you were cleansed; you were made holy; you were made right with God by calling on the name of the Lord Jesus Christ and by the Spirit of our God.*

BUT we were cleansed...
we were made holy...
we were made right with God by....
calling on the name of the Lord Jesus Christ and by the Spirit of our God!!!!!!!!

Oh dear one if you are in Jesus, if you have invited the Son of God to live in your heart then may your confidence be reaffirmed that the old has gone and the new is here by His redeeming grace!! Please record 2 Corinthians 5:17 below.

_____

_____

As we let that Truth marinate within us please reflect on what God spoke the loudest to your heart today from your study and how you might live that Truth out.

_____

_____

_____

_____

Day 5: The Most Beautiful Pathway

Welcome beloved of God. I am trusting you have already prayed. I'm praying Psalm 32:8 (NIV) over us all and clinging to its promise. *I will instruct you and teach you in the way you should go; I will counsel you with my loving eye on you.*

Walk with me a moment down this road…

- Romans 3:10 (NIV) *As it is written: "There is no one righteous, not even one;*

- Romans 3:23 (NIV) *for all have sinned and fall short of the glory of God*

- Romans 6:23 (NIV) *For the wages of sin is death, but the gift of God is eternal life in Christ Jesus our Lord.*

- Romans 5:8 (NIV) *But God demonstrates his own love for us in this: While we were still singers, Christ died for us.*

- Romans 10:9-10 (NIV) *If you declare with your mouth, "Jesus is Lord," and believe in your heart that God raised him from the dead, you will be saved. For it is with your heart that you believe and are justified, and it is with your mouth that you profess your faith and are saved.*

- Romans 10:13 (NIV) *for, "Everyone who calls on the name of the Lord will be saved."*

- John 3:16-17 (NIV) *For God so loved the world that he gave his one and only Son, that whoever believes in him shall not perish but have eternal life. For God did not send his Son into the world to condemn the world, but to save the world through him.*

- Romans 5:1-2 (NIV) *Therefore, since we have been justified through faith, we have peace with God through our Lord Jesus Christ, through whom we have gained access by faith into this grace in which we now stand. And we boast in the hope of the glory of God.*

- Romans 8:1 (NIV) *Therefore, there is now no condemnation for those who are in Christ Jesus,*

Beautiful, just beautiful Truth to tuck into our hearts. Do you know anyone that might need you to share this pathway with them?

In Jesus we have been cleansed which is a metaphor for the righteousness that comes by forgiveness.

Please read Acts 22:16 _____ and Titus 3:5. _____

We are made holy. Please read 1 Corinthians 1:2. _____

We are made right with God by way of our identification with Jesus and by the transforming work of the Holy Spirit.

Please read Romans 1:17 _____, and 3:21-26. _____

In Jesus we have been changed and we are forgiven and set free! We will still make mistakes but now we know those mistakes do not define us but remind us how much we need the ongoing love, grace and mercy of our Savior Jesus Christ. He is there without fail in overly abundant amounts of all that He is, and He never runs dry or short. Praise Him! May we ever choose to live to please and glorify Him!

he saved us, not because of righteous things we had done, but because of his mercy. He saved us through the washing of rebirth and renewal by the Holy Spirit, whom he poured out on us generously through Jesus Christ our Savior, so that, having been justified by his grace, we might become heirs having the hope of eternal life. Titus 3:5-7 (NIV)

I gave them eternal life, and they shall never perish; no one will snatch them out of my hand. John 10:28 (NIV)

Dearly beloved of God, I pray you know this Truth. Once you make the choice to believe in Jesus as Savior NOTHING can take you from His hand, NOTHING! You have the treasure of the Holy Spirit in you. You are now His vessel of Living Hope to the world!

Please close with 1 Corinthians 6:12-20. _____

1 Peter 2:12 (NLT) *Be careful to live properly among your unbelieving neighbors. Then even if they accuse you of doing wrong, they will see your honorable behavior, and they will give honor to God when he judges the world.*

You are dearly loved. Your life is a gift, purchased with the life of God's own Son. Carry the precious treasure of Him within you to a world longing to know the Truth upon which you stand -- unshaken.

Grace and peace~

Please record below this day's nugget of greatest impact to your heart.

_____
_____
_____
_____

But we have this treasure in jars of clay to show that this all-surpassing power is from God and not from us. We are hard pressed on every side, but not crushed; perplexed, but not in despair; persecuted, but not abandoned; struck down, but not destroyed. 2 Corinthians 4:7-9 (NIV)

Day 6 & 7: At His Feet – A Time to Reflect

Over the next two days take time to reflect over your week of study. Maybe you need some time to catch up on the study material and this might be the perfect break to do just that with the Lord!

I encourage you to glance back at the final point at the end of each day that you recorded having had the greatest impact on your heart. As you spend time with God in prayer, reflect and record on the lines below how God is tying it together and applying it to your life specifically for such a time as this.

Ask that God make it clear who He would have you invite into an opportunity to share Him, to apply what you are learning; maybe a child, grandchild, friend… trust Him to continue to take the lead. May we have a heart ever ready with eyes and ears out to the opportunities God wants to invite us into for His glory and praise.

Do not merely listen to the word, and so deceive yourselves. Do what it says. Anyone who listens to the word but does not do what it says is like someone who looks at his face in a mirror and, after looking at himself, goes away and immediately forgets what he looks like. But whoever looks intently into the perfect law that gives freedom, and continues in it – not forgetting what they have heard, but doing it – they will be blessed in what they do.
James 1:22-25 (NIV)

_____
_____
_____
_____
_____
_____
_____
_____
_____
_____

Philippians 4:13 (NIV) *I can do all this through him who gives me strength.*

John 14:26 (NIV) *But the Advocate, the Holy Spirit, whom the Father will send in my name, will teach you all things and will remind you of everything I have said to you.*

WEEK 8

Therefore go and make disciples of all nations, baptizing them in the name of the Father and of the Son and of the Holy Spirit, and teaching them to obey everything I have commanded you. And surely I am with you always, to the very end of the age."
Matthew 28:19-20 (NIV)

Day 1: Positive Force

Welcome to week 8! You certainly have taken up His positive force within to continue with such endurance! I greatly admire your tenacity. 2 Corinthians 5:14 (NIV) begins, *For Christ's love compels us,* Keep going dear one! Hebrews

11:6 (NIV) finishes, *he rewards those who earnestly seek him.*

May we begin this week in His Word together, bowed before Him asking that God Almighty lead us as He works on our hearts to follow Him wholeheartedly.

Colossians 1:29 (NIV) *To this end I strenuously contend with all the energy Christ so powerfully works in me.*

In the verse below who's name would you insert for Solomon's to make it more personal?

_____

1 Chronicles 29:19 (NLT)
Give my son Solomon the wholehearted desire to obey all your commands, laws, and decrees, and to do everything necessary to build this Temple, for which I have made these preparations."

Please begin by reading the following passages.
Matthew 12:1-8 _____, Mark 2:23-28 _____ and Luke 6:1-5. _____

This grouping of passages (above) records the Pharisees upset with what?
_____
It seems pointing fingers, finding fault in others and becoming a tattletale is not something contained to our generation and yet, He loves us anyway! Praise His redeeming grace His love is too strong to leave us that way!!

The Pharisees were determined to accuse Jesus of wrongdoing. What you look for, you generally find. When they saw Jesus allowing what they had determined should not be done on the Sabbath they were fired up and ready to make their accusation!

What do you generally look for in situations and circumstances? If you can take note of what you generally see it is probably a good indicator of what you look for. Are you most likely to see the good, the opportunity or the negative and the roadblocks?

_____

We can pray for eyes and ears attuned to His presence, His amazing grace and how He is working all things for good in every situation and circumstance.

How does Jesus respond to the Pharisees (specifically in Matthew 12:3-8)?

_____

Jesus AGAIN points them to the Scriptures (are you seeing this recurring theme too?!) If Jesus was always going back to the Scriptures... so should we be.

Please read 1 Samuel 21:1-6. _____

This Scripture records this event Jesus is referring to in our gospel readings today.

Verse 6 in 1 Samuel 21 (NLT) calls this bread what?

_____

The Bread of the Presence was 12 loaves of bread, probably to represent the 12 tribes of Israel (Gen. 49), which was brought each Sabbath into the Holy Place of the Tabernacle by a priest and only for the on duty priest. The bread was to represent God's presence and loving care of provision for His people's physical needs. (*NLT Study Bible* notes, pg. 497) (*Life Application Study Bible* notes, pg. 497)

Ahimelech the on-duty priest gave of his portion. How willing are we to give of "our portion" for the sake of another? When what the bread represented falls deep into our hearts it will become easier to let go of "our portion" for the sake of another because our Bread of Life never runs out of provision for us. We only have because He first gave us. *"No one can receive anything unless God gives it from heaven.* (John 3:27 NLT) We can never outgive God.

The Bread of the Presence had been replaced fresh the very day David and his men came with their need! The timing was perfect! Dear one, His all sufficient presence waits afresh each day for you and I!!

Do we try to bring Him our fresh best each day? Do we reverence our quiet time in His presence as a divine appointment? How do we show gratitude for the offer of His fresh Word to satisfy our hunger daily?

_____

_____

As God had not passed judgment on David for eating the Bread of the Presence Jesus was trying to point the Pharisees to His greater purpose in His response to their accusations. "Jesus was not condoning disobedience to God's laws. Instead, he was emphasizing discernment and compassion in enforcing the laws."[xiii] His disciples were not working to harvest for money; they were picking it because they were hungry.

Matt. 12:7 tells us God desires _____ over sacrifices. (mercy)

Can you recall a time when you needed to realize the bigger picture or purpose for the rule or regular way of doing things in order to move beyond it to fulfill that purpose behind it… mercifully?

_____

_____

Please record Matthew 12:8 below.

_____

What does that mean to you?

_____

_____

We may KNOW He is Lord over all, but do we reverence that fact in our heart so much that it impacts the outflow of our words, thoughts and actions?

Isaiah 45:9 brings this to a very personal level. What does this verse say we really have no right to do?

_____

As His creation, fearfully and wonderfully made (Ps 139:14) who are we to complain about how He made us?! He does a good job EVERY time! YOU are His bright idea to the world to carry forth His Light in just His perfect way!

Let us look at how God uses a circumstance that many would have considered unfortunate, but God used as the most fortunate opportunity to magnify Himself to a desperate world!

Please read Matthew 12:9-15 _____, Mark 3:1-6 _____ and Luke 6:6-11. _____

Again, we find the religious elite looking for ways to do away with Jesus, but Jesus (as always) was a zillion steps ahead of them and knew their thoughts.

Who happened to be at the synagogue that day while Jesus was preaching? A man with something out of the ordinary; sketch the scene briefly with your words.

_____

Do the things that we think are wrong with ourselves or our lives keep us from Jesus or draw us to Him?

This man, despite His life's hardship had drawn near to the presence of Jesus and received restoration. John 11:25 tells us Jesus is the resurrection and the life! There is no life or situation too far gone that He cannot redeem and restore. Oh, praise His redeeming grace!!

Mark 3:5 indicates Jesus looked around angrily and was deeply saddened by their hard hearts. It is not a sin to feel angry, it can turn into a sin depending on what you DO with your anger. Jesus did what in His anger (Mark 3:5)?

_____

He healed and restored!!

If the motives of our heart align with Jesus', then what angers Him will anger us and will motivate us to use that as a positive force to bring about His will His way! When was the last time your anger motivated you to heal and restore that which was broken in your life… maybe a relationship that needed an extension of forgiveness or an "I'm sorry", maybe a bitterness let go of?

In Luke 6:6-11 we see this man with a deformity was asked to stand before everyone and hold forth his shortcoming. When have we too been asked to obey and walk forward with God in our weakness so that the display of His strength could be made known? Were you willing to obey like this man?

_____

Please record 2 Corinthians 12:9 below.

_____

_____

Thank you so very dearly for joining me today. Please record what impacted your heart the most today.

_____

_____

_____

_____

Day 2: An Unfamiliar Way

Hello my friend. I do not know about you, but I'm a fan of spontaneous adventure… especially the ones I can plan down to every perfectly over analyzed and outlined detail. Gratefully God has saved me from my own obsessive control puddle by giving me six beautiful children! What better way to cause someone to have to rely on the great, I AM more than you will ever need for more than you'll ever plan, than to take them down the unfamiliar pathway of raising a child!

Praise God for the unfamiliar pathways that lead to the greatest unexpected blessings. Please bow in prayer with grateful hearts that in all our unknowns we know Who we can trust to be the Way in, through, and above it all.

Go ahead dear one and savor the following passages.
Matthew 12:15-21 _____, Mark 3:7-12 _____ and Luke 6:17-19. _____

Jesus was growing in popularity. He was healing everyone, and the enemy was clear on who He was even if it was still a question in many people's minds. What does Mark 3:11 record the enemy declaring Him to be?

_____

(NIV) *"You are the Son of God."*

Jesus wanted to show the people in His way and in His time just Who He was as there was much misconception regarding the type of Messiah they were expecting.

What does Matthew 12:18-21 tell us Jesus fulfilled recorded in Isaiah 42:1-4?

_____

_____

Matthew 12:21 (NLT) *And his name will be the hope of all the world."* He is our Living Hope beyond the grave!
How do you deal with things when God works in ways you least expect? Are you willing to be pliable and receptive to His will and way or do you fight it holding to an attitude of entitlement?

When our present circumstances are a resounding negative and seem to be so loud and in our face, it is not easy to be willingly pliable to what we would not choose. Like a fisherman we need to continue to cast and cast again ourselves and our cares on to Him (1 Peter 5:7). Allowing the heart ache and disappointments of this world to draw us nearer to the One that has experienced it all and understands how we feel and is the All Sufficient One to meet our hearts greatest need (Hebrews 4:14-16). The enemy would like nothing more than for us to fall away from the faith on account of all we do not understand rather than trust the faithful promises of our God (2 Cor. 2:10-11, 1 Cor. 13:12).

Maybe insert your name for "Israel" in Isaiah 42:16 (NLT) trusting our God to be ever faithful in all our unknowns. *I will lead blind Israel down a new path, guiding them along an unfamiliar way. I will brighten the darkness before them and smooth out the road ahead of them. Yes, I will indeed do these things; I will not forsake them.*

"To us who cry, 'It's not going to work,' the Lord lovingly says, 'Where is your faith? Haven't I promised you that everything is working together for good to those who love Me (Romans 8:28)? Haven't I promised you that I will bring you to a glorious end (Jeremiah 29:11)? Haven't I promised you that I will complete that which I've begun in you (Philippians 1:6)? Haven't I promised you that I will restore to you the years the locust has eaten (Joel 2:25)? Haven't I promised you that no weapon formed against you shall prosper (Isaiah 54:17)? Haven't I promised to supply all your need (Philippians 4:19), that if you seek Me first, everything will be added unto you (Matthew 6:33)?'"

(Courson, 2003, p. 344)[xiv]

What troubles God? The lack of faith in those that have heard His Truth. He is who He says He is, and He will bring about what He has promised in His Word.

1 Corinthians 2:9 (NIV) *However, as it is written: "What no eye has seen, what no ear has heard, and what no human mind has conceived" --the things God has prepared for those who love him--*

Dear one, may together we allow Him to lift our chin above our troubling, maybe even heart wrenching circumstance with His nail scarred hand that took our greatest tragedy from us. May He open our ears to hear His most compassionate whisper to our tenderest parts, John 14:1 (NASB*) "Do not let your heart be troubled; believe in God, believe also in Me.*

As we begin to wrap our study up today please turn to Mark 3:13-19 _____ and Luke 6:12-16. _____

Have you ever had to make a tough decision? Sometimes living out the tough decision to submit to a Christ-like attitude toward someone or something rather than a self-centered one is enough to send us over the edge of frustration, am I right?!

Here we see Jesus facing the task of pulling together His group of 12 which would eventually be the spark to which the bonfire of the gospel is ignited throughout the world as we know it today! This was no haphazard choosing, our passage in Luke tells us Jesus stayed up and prayed about this for how long?

_____

All night.

Have you ever spent the night in fervent prayer? I am sure those nights are not quickly forgotten. What has fervent prayer done for your relationship with your heavenly Father? How might we maintain an attitude of prayer even in times when we are not desperate for answers?

_____

Luke 6:13 tells us Jesus pulled together all His "disciples or, 'disciplined ones' - -those who were disciplined in learning and committed to studying--Jesus chose twelve apostles, or "sent out ones" as ambassadors to represent Him."(Courson, 2003, p. 326)[xv]

Remember how many He chose?

"Twelve being the number of government, twelve being the number of tribes in Old Testament Israel, in choosing twelve apostles, Jesus establishes the new government of the kingdom." (Courson, 2003, p. 326)[xvi]

How often do we spend time in prayer seeking Him to govern our thoughts, words and actions, or decisions and choices in life as opposed to pushing our own agenda and attempting to set up our own system that seems good to us and just asking for His stamp of approval?

May we remember just Who He is, the Lord of all, and reverence that in our hearts as we reflect on a few highlights from our recent study times.

- Delight yourself in Him. He is a God of fresh presence available to us daily.

- He is strong in our weakness and passionate for our eternal wellbeing. He is compassion and mercy, grace and forgiveness, healing and restoration.

- He is our Way in all familiar and unfamiliar pathways.

- God Almighty is a positive force moving all of time toward His Son's victorious return.

Dear one, I pray we allow Him to invade us with His positive force that we would be moved to walk with Him in heart, trusting that if He ever desires for our feet, mouth and or body to move as well, He will lead the way and we would faithfully follow.

Thank you muchly~ Please record the piece of our study today that had the most impact on your heart before signing off.

_____

_____

_____

_____

Day 3: Qualities of Distinction

Welcome! I am already blessed by you so thank you for the continued encouragement of your presence. Let us bow before the Almighty and pray once again that His faithful presence falls in a transforming way on our hearts and minds afresh with new insights, revelations and understandings from Him.

Proverbs 2:3-5 (NLT) is one to tuck into our hearts pocket. *Cry out for insight, and ask for understanding. Search for them as you would for silver; seek them like hidden treasures. Then you will understand what it means to fear the LORD, and you will gain knowledge of God.*

Today's study is dense in scripture, time with God should be one area in life that you do not feel pressure to rush through. Enjoy as you abide in Him. Go at the pace He sets for your hearts together.

This portion of scripture is known as Jesus' sermon on the mount and probably spanned over the course of a few days. Over our next few days of study together we are going to gather from these passages qualities of character that set us apart in Christ.

Today take time to familiarize yourself with the big overall picture these scriptures paint for us. In the days to follow we will zoom in that lens to take a more detailed look.

The One who carried our cross all the way to hell so that we could walk free deserves our obedience in walking the walk and talking the talk in sincerity and truth, bring noticeable contrast in this world to His glory, honor and praise.

In the same way, let your light shine before others, that they may see your good deeds and

141

glorify your Father in heaven. Matthew 5:16 (NIV)

You might want to make sure you have a warm cup of tea as you sit and savor the passages for today. Within each group of passages record one thing that really stands out to you in the following table as you read.

Jeremiah 33:3 (NIV) *'Call to me and I will answer you and tell you great and unsearchable things you do not know.'*

Matthew chapter 5 _____	
Matthew chapter 6 _____	
Matthew chapter 7 _____	
Luke 6:20-49 _____	

Thank you. Let God continue to speak to your heart through His living Word that you have planted in your heart as you go about your day today.

For the word of God is alive and active. Sharper than any double-edged sword, it penetrates even to dividing soul and spirit, joints and marrow; it judges the thoughts and attitudes of the heart. Hebrews 4:12 (NIV)

You have been recording impactful things all through todays study. What one thing can you narrow it down to that made the most impact on your heart today? Please record it below. God bless you muchly~

_____

_____

_____

_____

Day 4: Listen and Follow

Greetings dear one. I am so glad you have prioritized time with your Creator. *The Spirit of God has made me; the breath of the Almighty gives me life.* Job 33:4 (NIV)

Wind is such a powerful thing. Where I live the gusts can get powerful and it always inspires me to remember the Source! Though I cannot see the wind I see the mighty powerful effects of it. Though I may not see His face this side of heaven I see the effects of His almighty power. Though my physical eyes may be blinded at times, may He always open my spiritual eyes so that I would walk by faith in ever increasing trust. Begin in prayer dear one, that the Almighty might lead us to captivating depths of His heart today.

It will take nothing short of His Holy Spirit within us to live out the commands we have been studying. However, these commands are for our best life.

Matt. 7:24-27 and Luke 6:47-49 both depict for us an image of what a life looks like when we call on Him, listen to His teaching and then actually follow it.

Go ahead and humor me with a sketch of each scenario below according to the above scriptures.

143

Come, listen AND follow:	Hears but does not obey:

Being a visual learner myself that just has a bit stronger impact, see that analogy drawn out. It is not about knowing more as much as it is about being obedient with what you know.

Praise the One who is willing to fill us with all the fullness of His Spirit (Ephesians 3:19)! Record below the attributes the fruit of His Spirit. See Galatians 5:22-23.

_____

_____

Philippians 4:13 (ESV) *I can do all things through him who strengthens me.*

Yesterday I stated we were going to narrow our lens on these passages as the days went along. Yesterday you took time to read through our four-chapter segment of Scripture and recorded the one thing that most stood out to you from each chapter. Today you will take a more focused look at each section within each chapter and record that which impacts your heart the deepest, section by section, topic by topic.

Here is a list of areas we see addressed in these three chapters of Matthew. The ones with an asterisk next to them are areas that coincide with the passage in Luke.

*Beatitudes (Matt. 5:3-11; Lk. 6:20-26)	
Salt and Light (Matt. 5:13-16)	
The law (Matt. 5:17-20)	

Anger (Matt. 5:21-26)	
Adultery (Matt. 5:27-30)	
Divorce (Matt. 5:31-32)	
Vows (Matt. 5:33-37)	
Revenge (Matt. 5:38-42)	
*Love for enemies (Matt. 5:43-48; Lk. 6:27-36)	
Giving to the needy (Matt. 6:1-4)	
Prayer (Matt. 6:5-14)	
Fasting (Matt. 6:16-18)	
Money and Possessions (Matt. 6:19-24)	
Worry (Matt. 6:25-34)	

*Judgment (Matt. 7:1-5; Lk. 37-42)	
Wisdom (Matt. 7:6-12)	
Narrow Gate (Matt. 7:13-14)	
*Tree and fruit (Matt. 7:15-20; Lk. 6:43-45)	
True Disciples (Matt. 7:21-23)	
*Solid Foundation (Matt. 7:24-27; Lk. 6:46-49)	

Thank you sincerely for your effort in studying so diligently. Tomorrow I will share some of what stood out to me in the above passages but for now give what He has spoken directly to your heart time to marinate to perfection.

If you had to pick one point that sticks out in your mind most from all you have dug through today in His Word what would it be? Please record it below and maybe even add a practical way you feel Him leading you to live out that Truth.

_____
_____
_____
_____

Day 5: Meekness Not Weakness

Hello friend. Today we will continue studying qualities of distinction that appear in those set apart as authentically surrendered believers/followers of Jesus by the power of His Spirit within.

As we walk through these passages step by step once more please keep the notes God has given you directly the last two days in the forefront of your mind as we, in a way, combine our notes! First, let us pray that God be the pen that engraves His notes of Truth on the tablets of our hearts.

"This is the covenant I will make with them after that time, says the Lord. I will put my laws in their hearts, and I will write them on their minds." Hebrews 10:16 (NIV)

Let us begin pulling apart Matthew 5, 6, 7 and Luke 6:20-49!

Matthew 5:9 tells us blessed are what?

_____

Peacemakers or those who work for peace. Peace is the presence of His salvation.

Psalm 51:12 (NIV) *Restore to me the joy of your salvation and grant me a willing spirit, to sustain me.*

As disciples of Jesus we move toward justice, mercy, reconciliation, peace... as effects of our salvation and joy in Christ as His child. An example is Matt. 5:43-47, loving our enemies.

We are not in control of another's actions or reactions, but we are our own. Romans 12:18 tells us that as far as it depends on us to live at peace with all. This does not call for passiveness but rather a different kind of activism. The kind we see exemplified in the life of Jesus. Sometimes the strongest thing to do is exemplify gentleness, to have all the power in the world but choose to use it to lay aside your strength. Meekness is not weakness but incredible strength under control.

Matthew 5:11-12 tells us to be happy when we are persecuted... tell me that does not take all effects of His powerful and positive force within us!?!! The good side of persecution can be that it takes our eyes off earthly things and long for the perfection of heaven. It can strip us of a superficial faith in order to find that which is firm and True. The opportunity to exemplify God's character to a captive audience also often comes through persecution.

Can you think of a time you saw good come from a persecution you endured?

_____

_____

_____

Oh, praise His redeeming grace!

Matthew 5:20 talks of a different kind of righteousness. Not just living by the law but by the principles behind the law motivated by sincere reverence of our Heavenly Father.

Matthew 5:38 (NIV) begins, *"You have heard,* and verse 39 begins, *"But I tell you,* as many of the sections in these few chapters do. These Scriptures describe qualities that are distinctly not naturally human but supernatural. We must decide what we will let invade our heart, what we have heard from the world or what our God tells us. As you can see the two stand in stark contrast and the only way to fulfill these commands in sincerity and truth is by a full invasion of His Spirit within.

If we choose His filling people will take notice, you will have created a contrast; you will be salt and light but you will have had to follow His example and pick up your cross and die to yourself, die to your plans and your wants, you can't live for self and for God with ramped up effectiveness. Dying to self makes room for Him to live His best life in and through you to His glory and praise! This is life in abundance! It is completely backwards from the world's message of self-glorification. Living for self only leaves a void of Grand Canyon proportions. It is only in losing ourselves that we can gain the fullness of Christ and find we are truly alive. (John 10:10)

Philippians 1:20-21 (NIV) *I eagerly expect and hope that I will in no way be ashamed, but will have sufficient courage so that now as always Christ will be exalted in my body, whether by life or by death. For to me, to live is Christ and to die is gain.*

Matthew 6:4 talks about giving privately. Do we do our acts of generosity for us to look good or for God to look good? Ask yourself would I do this even if no one ever found out, would I care if someone else got the credit? It is easy to start thinking our vision is His will. Psalm 139:24-25 is a good prayer to pray asking that God give our hearts a motive check (rather than trying to do it ourselves as we may be a bit biased) but then we need to be open to obeying His leading and revelation.

Whatever you do, work at it with all your heart, as working for the Lord, not for human masters, Colossians 3:23 (NIV) *Search me, God, and know my heart; test me and know my anxious thoughts. See if there is any offensive way in me, and lead me in the way everlasting.* Psalm 139:23-24 (NIV)

The Our Father prayer is listed in Matthew 6:9-13. The two verses address Him and the last three are directed toward us… give us our daily bread, forgive us… It is important to keep first things, first. When we keep Him first in all compartments of our lives things just fit a whole lot better.

What are some of the compartments of your life? How do you allow God to infiltrate and take first in all of them or how could you invite Him up to some of the areas maybe you have left Him out of or have let Him slip slide down the list of importance?

_____

_____

_____

Job 22:21 (NIV) *"Submit to God and be at peace with him; in this way prosperity will come to you.*

Moving to Matthew 6:16-18. Again, the issue of true motives is brought up. What motivates our acts of faith? To be noticed and applauded by people or God? Nehemiah in chapter 13 of Nehemiah, verses 14, 22, 29 all record him crying out to God to remember his good deeds and his work on His behalf and even the wrongs done. Nehemiah sought God's approval and valued His authority and opinion above man's.

Am I now trying to win the approval of human beings, or of God? Or am I trying to please

people? If I were still trying to please people, I would not be a servant of Christ.
Galatians 1:10 (NIV)

What does the Lord require of you? What does He NOT require of you? Before responding please read Micah 6:6-8.

_____

_____

What does this look like practically in your life today?

_____

_____

Matthew 6:24 states no one (not some people - NO ONE) can serve two, what?

_____

No one can serve two masters! As much as this world applauds busy multitaskers, we cannot serve God that way. Nothing can come before Him, not even a little bit, not even at times. All the time God must take number one seat in your life and mine. It is the only way we will have spiritual eyes that are able to see with clarity. We must walk by faith, not sight or feeling. Faith requires trust and if that is divided, we will not have what it takes to step out where He wants to take us in Him.

Matthew 6:25-34 centers on worry. God knew many would allow worry to be used as an effective weapon against us, so He uses various illustrations to emphasize the uselessness of worry. Fill in the blanks below paraphrasing in your own words.

Verse 25 - Life is more than

_____

Also see 1 Cor. 15:55-57.

Verse 26 - Look at the birds they do not what, and yet what still happens?

_____

Also see Phil. 4:19.

Verse 27 - Does worry add moments to your life?   Yes or No

Verse 28 - Look at the lilies of the field and how they grow... what do you notice?

_____

_____

Would you ever guess that a bright yellow dandelion, one of those flowers that just look like sunshine rained down on earth would ever turn into a beautiful soft ball full of wishes?! Only God could bring a heart full of hope through what society would deem as a dead weed. Praise His redeeming grace!

Verse 32 assures us that our Heavenly Father knows what?

_____

_____

Luke 12:32 (NLT) *"So don't be afraid, little flock. For it gives your Father great happiness to give you the Kingdom.*

Matthew chapter 7 begins with the topic of judgment. Why do you think certain shortcomings stand out so blatantly in others? Could it be because we have fallen in the same area and are so familiar with such a struggle too? Might we give of the overflowing grace He has so lavished on us (2 Cor. 9:14). Using any authority He has given us to build others up rather than to tear them down (2 Cor. 10:8).

Matthew 7:7-11 addresses the effectiveness of prayer. As we pray, our heart's desire and delight, over time, conforms to be more like His. Our desires and requests begin to align more to His heart's. This passage addresses how a good father would answer their child's request with good things. Know that what our Heavenly Father answers our prayers with is always the absolute best. (Job 22:21)

The Golden Rule in Matthew 7:12 is characterized by a doing rather than a not doing. It seems this is a proactive command. Do not wait for a moment to repay good for good just give the good away to delight the Father's heart. What are some things you think you could do for another of His children that would delight the Father's heart?

_____

_____

_____

Matthew 7:21 (NLT) *"Not everyone who calls out to me, 'Lord! Lord!' will enter the Kingdom of Heaven. Only those who actually do the will of my Father in heaven will enter.*

Matthew 7:29 denotes that Jesus spoke with true authority. He Himself is the Word as He is the true foundation. As we stand on, and live from the solid foundation of His Word, depicting the Truth of His Way, we will exemplify distinctive qualities of His positive force as well, bringing reviving salt and light to a desperate world.

Whew!! Thank you for your diligent study of His Word today dear one. I believe after this week we may be quite pruned up with the Living Water of His Word! Nothing like a pruned up wrinkly heart from soaking in His Truth! Those wrinkles are the kind of tread that creates traction, making life a bit easier to navigate.

Please record how God impacted your heart most today while emersed in His Truth.

_____

_____

_____

_____

Day 6 & 7: At His Feet – A Time to Reflect

Over the next two days take time to reflect over your week of study. Maybe you need some time to catch up on the study material and this might be the perfect break to do just that with the Lord!

I encourage you to glance back at the final point at the end of each day that you recorded having had the greatest impact on your heart. As you spend time with God in prayer, reflect and record on the lines below how God is tying it together and applying it to your life specifically for such a time as this.

Ask that God make it clear who He would have you invite into an opportunity to share Him, to apply what you are learning; maybe a child, grandchild, friend... trust Him to continue to take the lead. May we have a heart ever ready with eyes and ears out to the opportunities God wants to invite us into for His glory and praise.

Do not merely listen to the word, and so deceive yourselves. Do what it says. Anyone who listens to the word but does not do what it says is like someone who looks at his face in a mirror and, after looking at himself, goes away and immediately forgets what he looks like. But whoever looks intently into the perfect law that gives freedom, and continues in it – not forgetting what they have heard, but doing it – they will be blessed in what they do.
James 1:22-25 (NIV)

_____

_____

_____

_____

_____

_____

_____

_____

_____

Philippians 4:13 (NIV) *I can do all this through him who gives me strength.*

John 14:26 (NIV) *But the Advocate, the Holy Spirit, whom the Father will send in my name, will teach you all things and will remind you of everything I have said to you.*

WEEK 9
And the peace of God, which transcends all understanding, will guard your hearts and minds in Christ Jesus. Philippians 4:7 (NIV)

Day 1: The Opportunity of Interruption
Hello, thanks for coming today. The fact that you have made it this far shows distinctive character traits of enduring diligence to finish what you start. This reflects the Fathers heart displayed in Philippians 1:6. In fact, maybe allow Philippians 1:3-6 (NIV) to start our beginning prayer today. *I thank my God every time I remember you. In all my prayers for all of you, I always pray with joy because of your partnership in the gospel from the first day until now, being confident of this, that he who began a good work in you will carry it on to completion until the day of Christ Jesus.*

As we gaze through the following windows of Scripture, we won't want to miss catching a glimpse of one such a Roman officer who chose to exemplify distinctive qualities of a firm faith.

Meet you on the other side of Matthew 8:5-13 _____ and Luke 7:1-10. _____

This Roman (a Gentile) displayed extreme faith. How?

_____

He allowed faith to trump his sight and quite possibly his feelings. He needed to let go of worry and doubt to cling to trust like he did. What was the result of his faith (verse 13)?

_____

Does this always mean that we will get what we want, when we want, how we want, if only we believe? No. God understands things we do not and sees things we cannot. Are we placing our faith and trust in an outcome or in the good God of the outcome?

In Luke 7:4 it is clear everyone thinks this man deserves God's good favor yet the centurion states in verse 6-7 he clearly does NOT feel he deserves God's favor. He does not even feel worthy to come to Jesus, but he had faith enough to know, to KNOW, that if Jesus spoke the word, favor would be shown to him and his family.

Luke 7:9 finds Jesus amazed... the God of the universe AMAZED can you believe it?! Amazed at what?

_____

The centurion's great faith! Faith to believe in just who He was, a good and faithful God of amazing grace!

God help us to put our faith and trust in WHO you promise to faithfully be to us in and through all circumstances. That in all things you are working for the good of those that love you (Romans 8:28) and not to fall away because we don't see or understand how and what You are doing (1 Cor. 13:12). Help our hearts not to worry and to not be troubled but to cast it all on Your strong heart and shoulders (John 14:1,27, 1 Peter 5:7, Matthew 11:30).

Matthew 24:13 (NIV) *but the one who stands firm to the end will be saved.*

In Matthew 8:5 the Roman officer visited Jesus, Luke 7:3 says he sent people in his place. Dealing with a person's messengers was the same as dealing with the one who sent them in those days.

In this passage we see Jesus crossing artificial barriers. Different racial and religious backgrounds are represented here and yet Jesus moves right through to heal the Roman's servant. How willing are we to cross differences to unite in the Truth of Jesus?

_____

Keep reading a bit further in Luke. Luke 7:11-17. _____

Our God has power over life and death. Please read John 11:25-26. How does this Scripture encourage you?

_____

_____

Luke 7:13 (NLT) tells us, *his heart overflowed with compassion.* Jesus, during His travels to Nain did not become frustrated with the procession in His way but rather was moved with compassion to the point He interceded!

When was the last time you encountered a delay, distraction or an interruption to your day or agenda, and you saw it rather as an opportunity!? An opportunity for your heart to respond and intervene with sincere compassion. An opportunity to step out in faith and trust in order to magnify His heart to those around you. An opportunity to exemplify distinctive qualities that only come from His Spirit within?! Take a moment to respond below.

_____

_____

_____

You may be very good at seeing interruptions as opportunities and maybe not but remember the hope tied up in the Truth of Lamentations 3:22-23 (NIV) *Because of the LORD's great love we are not consumed, for his compassions never fail. They are new every morning; great is your faithfulness.*

Praise Him for never seeing us as an interruption so that He can be with us in all opportunities He brings our way.

Please record what made the most impact on your heart today.

_____

_____

_____

_____

Day 2: The Fence of Offences

Hi! Are you ready for our divine appointment with the God of the Universe?! First, we pray.

Meet you on the other side of Matthew 11:1-19 _____ and Luke 7:18-35. _____

Matthew 11:2 tells us John is hearing about all that Jesus is doing from where?!

_____

In prison! Remember who John is?! Remember He is a relative of Jesus, the miraculous child of Zechariah and Elizabeth, the one who has given his life faithfully to prepare the way for Jesus!!! And he is where?! In PRISON?!

It seems John is just as confused about the way his life is playing out because what question does he send his buddies out to ask Jesus in verse Matt. 11:3?

_____

Now remember John is the same guy who baptized Jesus and saw the sky rip open to the audible voice of God Himself declaring His pleasure over His one and only Son Jesus! Yet John asks from prison if maybe he got it wrong… because if Jesus was it, why would he be in prison?!

Have you ever thought you were owed a different ending than that which was or did occur in life?

_____

_____

Dear one, He DID give us a better ending. For those of us that believe in Jesus, this here and now on earth is the worst we will ever endure - we have a Kingdom Paradise awaiting us as our true home. Jesus gave His very life to afford us a different ending. Let us pray that an attitude of offended entitlement does not trip us up from our eternal destination.

In response to John's question in verse 3, Jesus tells them in Matthew 11:4 to report what they have already seen and heard.

How have you already seen and heard His faithfulness in your own life?

_____

_____

For as far back as I can remember my dad always instructed me with the advice, "Go back to what you know." Go back to what you know, go back to when it made sense, then work forward from there. I believe the first time he may have told me that was over some frustrating math homework, but it is wise advice that applies to all of life if you think about it.

Here, in response to John's ponderings I think Jesus is saying, remember what you know is Truth. Go back to what you know and work forward from there. Remember what you have seen and heard and remember the Truth of the Scriptures to help you find your bearings in times of trial. Go back to what you know to find your faith in all that you don't.

How might you apply this advice to your own confusing situations and circumstances?

_____

_____

_____

Okay, now what does Jesus point them to in Matthew 11:5?

_____

Scripture being fulfilled! Compare Matthew 11:5 to Isaiah 35:4-6; 42:7, 18; 61:1.

Matthew 11:6 holds such a great reminder for me. Please record that verse below.

_____

When we are overwhelmed with the unknown, unexplainable and unthinkable turn to the Scriptures. You will find your Faithful and True foundation unshaken and sustaining.

Isaiah 41:13 (NIV) *For I am the LORD your God who takes hold of your right hand and says to you, Do not fear; I will help you.*

Let us pray to...

- Be flexible and pliable in the Master's hand.

- Take time to remember what we have already witnessed to be True about Him, remembering the Scriptures.

- Pray against becoming cynical or skeptical because His Word and Way may challenge us to move from our self-centered lifestyle into His life. We'll find life abundant when we are willing to die to ourselves. This will take character qualities of distinction that will only point to our Heavenly Father as the Source of all that enables us to rise above. For He Himself is our victory.

God's word is unchained (2 Timothy 2:9) and free for all however in order to truly *receive* it, it's going to cost our attitude of offended entitlement, our stubborn heart, our self-righteous attitude…

Let's not let the enemy trip us up with the ol' fence trick!! Those of-fences can really cause quite a fall if we are not careful!

Luke 7:35 (NLT) *But wisdom is shown to be right by the lives of those who follow it.*

Thank you muchly. He will honor your faithfulness, your sincere effort to draw ever nearer to His heart.

Please record your greatest impact from today.

_____

_____

"For my thoughts are not your thoughts, neither are your ways my ways," declares the LORD. *"As the heavens are higher than the earth, so are my ways higher than your ways and my thoughts than your thoughts.* Isaiah 55: 8-9 (NIV)

And we know that in all things God works for the good of those who love him, who have been called according to his purpose. Romans 8:28 (NIV)

Jesus replied, "You do not realize now what I am doing, but later you will understand." John 13:7 (NIV)

That is why I am suffering as I am. Yet this is no cause for shame, because I know whom I have believed, and am convinced that he is able to guard what I have entrusted to him until that day. 2 Timothy 1:12 (NIV)

Day 3: Gripe to Grin

Hello my dear friend. Welcome back, have you had time yet for all that we dug through yesterday to settle in your heart? I am trusting God to continue to work it out in me, to will and to act according to His good purpose (Phil. 2:13). Let us bow before our Leader and ask that He continue to uncover great and unsearchable things we do not know (Jer. 33:3).

Please begin with Matthew 11:20-24. _____

Remember Jesus' response to John's question back in Matt. 11:3-5? You may even want to glance at the end of yesterday's notes.

The miracles Jesus performed confirmed without a doubt He was and is the Messiah the Scriptures point to. To reject the Truth results in death and destruction of which is our path to choose. The free gift of eternal life is held out to all of us (John 3:16).

Some of the towns in this Matthew passage had a reputation of wickedness. No matter how long standing the generational strongholds of wickedness may be in your family line, today YOU can be the signpost of a new way, The Way.

Please record Psalm 27:1 below.

_____

_____

Please travel further into Matthew chapter 11. Verses 25-30. _____

Verse 27 reveals the unity between the Father and the Son and an example of the relationship He wants with us. John 17:21 (NIV) *that all of them may be one, Father, just as you are in me and I am in you. May they also be in us so that the world may believe that you have sent me.*

Matthew 11:29 uses the metaphor of a yoke to illustrate true discipleship. Jesus' yoke is not less demanding but rather is carried in the strength of the Messiah. Verse 29 indicates our Teacher, our Leader to which we are yoked is humble and gentle at heart. Jesus' yoke is not easier however when Who you are yoked with has limitless strength, energy and wisdom that yoke becomes bearable. A gripe turned to grin!

Is there any burden you have been trying to shoulder alone that you need to allow yourselves to exchange for His yoke, set over a bigger stronger set of shoulders?

_____

_____

Dear one, please check out Numbers 21:4-9. _____
It seems the people of Israel had no problem expressing their poor attitudes of unappreciation. They resented the provision God was providing them, so God backed off and gave them over to themselves.

How do you feel when you are unappreciated? It is not appreciated! God does not appreciate it either. He will never force our love and acceptance of Him. That would not be true love.

What happens in Numbers 21:6?

_____

God allowed the poisonous snakes to attack. YET in His amazingly redemptive grace and mercy He provides what, in verses 8-9?

_____

A way to be saved!!! A way to repent and acknowledge their need of Him!

John 3:14-15 references this event. Please check out that address and then record John 3:16-17 below.

_____
_____
_____

So much hope! Jesus is our opportunity for salvation, life and new chances!

John 12:32 tells us that when Jesus is lifted up, He will draw all people to Himself! He is a God above all sickness, disease, depression, oppression, tragedy… He is a God that has overcome and we are to lift Him up so that all the world can see! Those that are weary and heavy laden can come to Him, believe in Him and rest in His salvation (Matt. 11:28)!! That my friend is hope, living hope on every page of your life!!

Jesus answered, "I am the way and the truth and the life. No one comes to the Father except through me. John 14:6 (NIV)

Please record the point of greatest impact to your heart today dear one. See you tomorrow!

_____
_____
_____
_____

Day 4: Seek and Pursue Peace

Welcome back my friend. Let us jump right back in where we left off yesterday. But first… pray.

Savor Luke 7:36 - 8:3. _____

Working from the back end of this passage (8:2-3) we see that Jesus allowed women to travel and learn from Him (not the norm for that time). Thus indicating that the different roles men and women fulfill do not denote worth.

They are different but equal in value to our God.

Our God gives overflowing hope (Romans 15:13) and overflowing grace (2 Cor. 9:14), what could overflow from our hearts but love for a God like that!

Luke 7:45 (NIV) (please fill in the blank) *You did not give me a kiss, but this woman, from the _____ __ _____, has not stopped kissing my feet.* (time I entered)

Goodness knows from the first moment God Almighty is welcomed into a heart there is life change! 2 Cor. 5:17 (NIV) *Therefore, if anyone is in Christ, the new creation has come: The old has gone, the new is here!* Tell me that does not turn a gripe to a song and a frown into the most giant grin!!
How deeply do you appreciate the width and depth of God's grace and mercy in your life? In the life of another? How does your life give evidence to your level of appreciation - daily?

_____

_____

Gratefully meet me on the other side of Matthew 12:22-37 _____, Mark 3:20-30 _____, and Luke 11:14-23. _____

Each of these passages finds Jesus accused of working with the opposite side. How easy is it for us to make excuses or call coincidence that which was divinely Him?! What does James 1:6 have to say about doubt?

_____

Jesus points out that any kingdom or even a family divided will fall! Jesus states only someone stronger than Satan could plunder his goods… thus making Him the stronger One!

Revelation 20:10 (NLT) *Then the devil, who had deceived them, was thrown into the fiery lake of burning sulfur, joining the beast and the false prophet. There they will be tormented day and night forever and ever.*

Oh, if we only had eyes that could physically see the spiritual battle going on all around us! Please read Colossians 2:15. _____

Is there anything wilder!! The enemy couldn't believe his eyes as he took in the empty tomb! The ultimate battle is won! Our God reigns forevermore! However, the battle is now on for our very souls! The enemy knows his time is short and will do anything to detour us from Truth and get us to fall away from the faith. What will the final population of heaven and hell be?! It is imperative that we remain in the victory of Jesus as we carry out our purposeful mission of pointing all to our Victor.

How does Mark 3:28 (NIV) begins, *Truly I tell you*, Jesus was always emphasizing the Truth by which He spoke!

He IS Truth (John 14:6)!

What does Luke 11:24-26 tell us we are in danger of if we do not purposely fill with Truth the empty gap left after expelling evil?

_____

Psalm 34:14 (NIV) *Turn from evil and do good; seek peace and pursue it.*

Please underline "Turn from" and "seek peace" then circle "do good" and "pursue it" in the above verse. Turn, seek, do and pursue…

God gives us something to do once we have expelled the lies from our mind… TURN away from evil, don't sit on the sidelines and watch or hang out with the same group of people that engage in what you know is not right. TURN and fix your gaze, time and energy elsewhere. Where? To DOING good! SEEKING peace! PURSUING it! That's enough to keep me busy and filled up with Truth leaving no room in my heart and mind for the enemy to set up camp again!

How might you implement this in a particular situation or circumstance in your life?

_____

_____

Reminder: WHO is Peace?
Check Ephesians 2:14.

Dear one may we seek and pursue Peace every day of our lives.

Matthew 12:31-32 addresses the unforgivable sin. What is it?
_____

It is rejecting God. It's not that one sin is worse and unforgivable; it's that rejecting the one force that pulls you toward God, the Holy Spirit, removes yourself from One that can save you! You must believe to receive the gift of eternal life.

Luke 11:28 (NLT) states, *Jesus replied, "But even more blessed are all who hear the word of God and put it into practice."*

Please underline, "...and put it into practice." As we go out today please take a moment and list at least three ways you can put into practice that which you have heard in the Word of God.

Consider:
How might I believe a word of Truth and not doubt? How might I receive His peace? How might I yoke myself to Him learning from His gentle and humble strength. How might we rise above false accusations or turn from evil and TO Truth? It will take the strength of the One who is strongER!

1.) _____
2.) _____
3.) _____

1 John 4:4 (NIV) *You, dear children, are from God and have overcome them, because the one who is in you is greater than the one who is in the world.*

Go in His strength dear one and thank you sincerely for studying with me today!

Please record the point of greatest impact.
_____
_____
_____

Day 5: Extend the Family

Hello my friend! Welcome! It is the delightful season of spring on the edge of summer from where I stand today. It is one of those sweet evenings after a thunderstorm that holds all the crispness of clean earth, cool air and the fresh sweet lilac sent awakened like only His rain can do.

The storm passed just in time to get a family grill in, complete with all the trimmings of ice cream mustaches and sticky watermelon grins. My heart is full as I settle in (with maybe just one more slice of watermelon). Knowing that in His family there is room and provisions for us all and a seat at His banqueting table for each of us who have accepted the invitation to be part of His family and live is pure joy!

Praise our good Father and ask that He stir up our heart to crave more of Who He is and a desire to follow His lead with joyful enthusiasm.

A verse to tuck into our hearts pocket: Romans 8:15 (NIV) *The Spirit you received does not make you slaves, so that you live in fear again; rather, the Spirit you received brought about your adoption to sonship. And by him we cry, "Abba, Father."*

Please meet me on the other side of Matthew 12:38-45. _____

What was it the religious leaders wanted more of to be convinced Jesus was the Messiah? (verse 38)

Miraculous signs. Could they have been looking rather for signs that they could use against Him? Were they already so convinced of what they thought they knew that their hearts had become hardened to any opportunity they had to find Truth?

It is easy to allow our own finite understanding to cloud His greater wisdom right out of our minds.

Proverbs 3:5-6 (NIV) *Trust in the LORD with all your heart and lean not on your own understanding; in all your ways submit to him, and he will make your paths straight.*

In His Word we all have the proof we need if we will just open our hearts even just a crack to let the Light come in and take root. Believe and move forward. Jesus' birth, life, death and resurrection as the fulfillment of Scripture are proof enough of His love and Godship.

Jesus points these questioning religious leaders back again to the Scriptures and the signs given in the Old Testament that point to Him. In the book of Jonah, Jonah spent three days and three nights inside the belly of a whale (Jonah 1:17) just as Jesus would spend three days in the tomb before resurrecting.

Jesus points to how the entire city of Ninevah repented at the teaching of Jonah and He is greater than Jonah! He points to the Queen of Sheeba traveling far and wide to seek out the great wisdom of Solomon and now He has come as one even greater than Solomon and still they do not believe or repent! Have you ever missed a His message to your heart because you had become hardened to anything other than what you wanted to hear?

_____

_____

Have you ever missed out on an adventure with Him because you failed to trust Him with your present circumstance because you couldn't wrap your brain around the fact that maybe He was trying to be bigger than anything you could have wrapped a frame of reference around from your past?

_____

_____

How might we learn and move forward into Him, open to HIS message HIS way and allow Him to reframe a bigger portrait of Himself as we step out into deeper and wider oceans with Him? Taking what we already know and allowing Him to build a bigger box then the one we keep trying to put Him in. (Maybe even let go of the "box" all together and just trust Him to keep building you to His glory!)

_____

_____

_____

I think the key word here is TRUST. We must let go into the hands of Him who is Faithful and True.

Last group of readings today. Matthew 12:46-50 _____, Mark 3:31-35 _____, and Luke 8:19-21. _____

These passages touch on His true family. To be a part of His family you must believe in Who Jesus is according to the Bible.

Those who are true members of His family DO the will of the Father. Obedience does not earn you a spot in the family of God, but it is a natural outpouring of a child of God to want to obey God's commands. Remember what Matthew 7:21 stated? Please record it below.

_____

_____

Romans 8:14-16 (NIV) *For those who are led by the Spirit of God are the children of God. The Spirit you received does not make you slaves, so that you live in fear again; rather, the Spirit you received brought about your adoption to sonship. And by him we cry, "Abba, Father." The Spirit himself testifies with our spirit that we are God's children.*

Have you accepted your spot in His family? Have you made known to someone else that they too have a spot in His family?

What is God's will, His mission, for each one of us? Refer to Matthew 28:19-20.

_____

_____

Where do we start?

Start with the ground beneath your own two feet. Allow His positive force, His Spirit to ignite an enthusiasm for His Word through prayer within your heart. May we be pliable in His hand as He works out His qualities of distinction that belong to those of His family so that we can rejoice in all things (Phil. 4:4) replacing our gripe for a grin that reaches deep and wide into all hearts revealing their place in His family as He Himself knits their soul to eternity with Him. My dad says, "be someone that when others are around you, they feel they have just been hugged by Jesus."

So, who has He caused to enter your circle of influence right where you are at?

_____

As you walk with Him closely in your heart, just being faithful with where you are at with what you've been given, you can trust that in all your steps, and in all your stops, He stays. Praise Him!

Whether you turn to the right or to the left, your ears will hear a voice behind you, saying, "This is the way; walk in it." Isaiah 30:21 (NIV)

Please record what has made the greatest impact on your heart today. Thank you!

_____
_____
_____
_____

Jesus replied, "My light will shine for you just a little longer. Walk in the light while you can, so darkness will not overtake you. Those who walk in the darkness cannot see where they are going. Put your trust in the light while there is still time; then you will become children of the light." John 12:35-36 (NLT)

Day 6 & 7: At His Feet – A Time to Reflect

Over the next two days take time to reflect over your week of study. Maybe you need some time to catch up on the study material and this might be the perfect break to do just that with the Lord!

I encourage you to glance back at the final point at the end of each day that you recorded having had the greatest impact on your heart. As you spend time with God in prayer, reflect and record on the lines below how God is tying it together and applying it to your life specifically for such a time as this.

Ask that God make it clear who He would have you invite into an opportunity to share Him, to apply what you are learning; maybe a child, grandchild, friend… trust Him to continue to take the lead. May we have a heart ever ready with eyes and ears out to the opportunities God wants to invite us into for His glory and praise.

Do not merely listen to the word, and so deceive yourselves. Do what it says. Anyone who listens to the word but does not do what it says is like someone who looks at his face in a mirror and, after looking at himself, goes away and immediately forgets what he looks like. But whoever looks intently into the perfect law that gives freedom, and continues in it – not forgetting what they have heard, but doing it – they will be blessed in what they do.
James 1:22-25 (NIV)

_____
_____
_____
_____
_____
_____
_____
_____
_____
_____

Philippians 4:13 (NIV) *I can do all this through him who gives me strength.*

John 14:26 (NIV) *But the Advocate, the Holy Spirit, whom the Father will send in my name, will teach you all things and will remind you of everything I have said to you.*

WEEK 10
The Spirit and the bride say, "Come!" And let the one who hears say, "Come!" And let the one who is thirsty come; and let the one who wishes take the free gift of the water of life.
Revelation 22:17 (NIV)

Day 1: Strong and Trustworthy
Welcome dearly beloved of God. You made it! Quite an accomplishment to reach the end of book one in this four-part study of the life of Jesus! Very bittersweet for me. I have enjoyed our time together so very much under the leadership of God Almighty. I know we have gone deep into His Word and it has cost quite a deal of time and effort to prioritize your walk with Him over

these past ten weeks. God has seen every time you chose Him over all the distractions vying for your heart; each time you submitted to His strength in your weakness. Well done good and faithful servant (Matt. 25:23), He rewards those who earnestly seek Him (Heb. 11:6).

I pray that as you have diligently spent time emersed within the Light of His Truth that you have reaped a harvest of ever-increasing trust in the God who designed you, planned for you, still has great purpose for you and loves you beyond comprehension. I pray you have allowed Him to enrapture your heart more deeply in love with His and that a craving for more of Him has been stirred to a level that is most captivating and energizing!

I pray that even though this appears to be the ending it will in fact be only the beginning of a most thrilling adventure as you lay a firm foundation of trust in Him who is Faithful and True. May you allow Him to continue to build your faith up in the trustworthy Rock that He is as He continues to write your story (Eph. 2:10) to His glory (Matt. 5:16)!

Dear one, God always finishes what He starts and since you're still here with a breath in your lungs it's hard core proof that God's not done with your story yet (Job 12:10, Phil. 1:6)! (Neither are we! So, let us commit to finishing strong in our final week together!)

Job 12:10 (NIV) states, *In His hand is the life of every creature and the breath of all mankind.* Begin in prayer using our gift of the breath of life to praise the One who has brought us this far.

Then Samuel took a stone and set it up between Mizpah and Shen. He named it Ebenezer, saying, "Thus far the LORD has helped us." 1 Samuel 7:12 (NIV)

Let us raise our own "Ebenezer" but maybe we can call our raised rock "Trust"! For thus far the true Light of the world has helped us! Might we tuck this treasure into our heart's pocket for our journey today. TRUST, for *"Thus far the LORD has helped us!"*

We will wind our way back into the Old Testament today. Please read Joshua chapter 1. _____

This chapter begins with *"After the death…"*, only in Jesus can there be anything "after death".

1 Peter 1:3 (NIV) states, *Praise be to the God and Father of our Lord Jesus Christ! In his great mercy he has given us new birth into a living hope through the resurrection of Jesus Christ from the dead,*

Please underline "living hope" in that verse above. What does that mean to you?

_____

_____

In Joshua 1:1, after death, God spoke! God still speaks living hope into situations and circumstances that seem dead to us! Do we trust Him enough to walk through the valley of the shadow of death and not fear knowing Immanuel is God WITH us even in the darkest valley's?

Before you reflect on that trust question do you find it interesting that in Psalm 23:4 NKJV the valley is described as the SHADOW of death? A shadow is harmless but shroud in darkness it can create fear. I say "it" because God does not give us a spirit of fear.

What does He give us according to 2 Timothy 1:7?

_____

Where there is a shadow there MUST be light! The rest of Psalm 23:3 states the reason for no fear is that the psalmist trusts completely in God's faithful presence. May we too take hold of and trust the confident Truth declared in Psalm 23:4 walking fearless over any mountain and through any valley!

Psalm 23:4 NKJV begins, *Yea, though I walk through the valley of the shadow of death, I will far no evil; For You are with me;*

In Joshua chapter 1 we see God commissioning Joshua as the new leader.

Joshua will lead God's people into the Promised Land. The thing is the Promised Land is full of enemies. Is the enemy trying to claim what God has already declared to be yours in Him?

(Joshua 1:3 NLT) *Wherever you set foot, you will be on land I have given you*

Please circle the word "given" in that verse above. Joshua and company have yet to set foot into the battle and yet God has already declared their victory!!

Dear one you were made to carry His victory!! It starts with a firm foundation of TRUST. Trust that your Heavenly Father loved you enough to send His Son to be the sacrifice for your sin (and mine) that He became the Way to be made right with God and enter into the resting place of His salvation!

Jesus conquered sin, death and the devil and you and I were made to carry the victory into the world by His grace and for His glory! *But thanks be to God, who always leads us as captives in Christ's triumphal procession and uses us to spread the aroma of the knowledge of him everywhere.* 2 Corinthians 2:14 (NIV) You are not fighting for the victory any more than Joshua and company were. You fight from it! Do you trust Him to be your defender, your stronghold that cannot be shaken?!!

Psalm 18:2 (NIV) *I love you, LORD, my strength. The LORD is my rock, my fortress, and my deliverer; my God is my rock, in whom I take refuge, my shield and the horn of my salvation, my stronghold.*

In Joshua 1:5 God tells Joshua that no one will be able to stand against him. Why? Because God will be with him and God will not fail or abandon him.

Are we willing to move forward in trust knowing that God will be with us and neither fail nor abandon us either? Do we trust Him enough to surrender our expectations of how we think things should go so the Master Potter can create His best work with our lives?

Oftentimes it is within all we do not know or understand that we find something better we never even knew to look for! It seems in Scripture Jesus often used the storms and the questions and the interruptions, even the failed expectations to reveal lifesaving Truth far beyond what could have ever been asked or even imagined (Eph. 3:20)!

When we feel tossed in the waves of doubt, we need to drop our anchor right there in the middle of the storm knowing we were made for this! This very thing the enemy means to destroy you, can strengthen you in faith! Fix your eyes on the unshaken Living Hope whose victory you hold within. *This hope is a strong and trustworthy anchor for our souls.* (Hebrews 6:19 NLT)

What 3 instruction does God give Joshua in Joshua 1:8?

_____

_____

_____

Verse 8 in the NLT states it this way, *Study this Book of Instruction continually. Meditate on it day and night so you will be sure to obey everything written in it. Only then will you prosper and succeed in all you do.*
Study God's Word.
Day and night, may it be on the forefront of your mind.
Obey it.

When we immerse in God's Truth it begins to govern our thoughts which govern our emotions which then often results in our actions. It matters where we place our minds.

Romans 12:2 (NIV) *Do not conform to the pattern of this world, but be transformed by the renewing of your mind. Then you will be able to test and approve what God's will is – his good, pleasing and perfect will.*

Isaiah 26:3 (NIV) *You will keep in perfect peace those whose minds are steadfast, because they trust in you.*

Dear one, you have immersed yourself in God's Truth these past couple months so drop your anchor and raise your rock of TRUST! Go back to what you know to find your faith in all that you don't for … *"Thus far the LORD has helped us."*

He is strong and trustworthy today, tomorrow and forever! Praise Him as you record the point of greatest impact to your heart from today.

_____

_____

_____

_____

Joshua 1:9 (NIV) *Have I not commanded you? Be strong and courageous. Do not be afraid; do not be discouraged, for the LORD your God will be with you wherever you go."*

Day 2: Unshakable Peace

Hello friend. A favorite children's book of mine that I love to read to my children is about a lovable furry monster that is afraid of monsters. He believes at the end of the book there will be a monster and he is very afraid! So, he tries everything NOT to get to the end of the book. I read this book with a silly monster voice and have fun acting out the different things this little monster tries to do to prevent turning the pages. My mom used to read it to me just the same fun way so it is extra special to have such fun reading it to my own kids.

The reason I bring this up is because I think I sort of relate to that little furry monster not wanting to get to the end of this book right now! The closer we come to the end the more I want to linger. But you know, at the end of that sweet monster book that monster realized the only monster at the end of the book was him!! And you know what else?! When we get to the end of our book, we will still have Him, our Lord and Savior the faithful Light of our life!

As we praise our God for His faithful presence let us bend our knee and begin in prayer.

Looking back at the end of yesterday's study in Joshua 1:9 it lists two emotions NOT to be what are they?

_____

Do not be AFRAID or DISCOURAGED.

God knew some of the most effective weapons the enemy welds against us are fear and discouragement. In Joshua 1:9 what reasoning does God give for not being this way?

Do not BE afraid or discouraged because I will BE with you!! Where will you choose to BE?

Psalm 91:1-2 (NIV) states, *Whoever dwells in the shelter of the Most High will rest in the shadow of the Almighty. I will say of the LORD, "He is my refuge and my fortress, my God, in whom I trust."*

We have a dwelling place to BE, right there in the Most High! Please circle the phrase "will rest" in the above verses and underline "my God, in whom I trust."

You can't be afraid and discouraged and still be at rest. Again, we see TRUST is the key. Trust leads to resting (not a hot mess of fearful discouragement). Trusting our God allows us to just BE in Him which warrants REST so we can truly LIVE and live VICTORIOUS!

How different our life's circumstances appear when our minds and bodies are rested. Before we dive into Joshua 2 please glance back once again to Joshua 1:13. What will the LORD God give according to this verse?

Rest. Rest on every level can only come from God. Rest physically, emotionally, financially, socially… The waves of a storm can rage, and yet the child of God can rest secure on every level via the root of trust.

Swing on over to Hebrews and please read Hebrews 4:1-11. _____

Did you notice verse 8 in that no human could or can provide the kind of restful peace the Prince of Peace can. Those who put (that's an action under our control – to put) their trust in the sure foundation of His faithful promises will find rest in their day to day moments.

This is not all!! For those of us in Jesus, those who have recognized their sinfulness and their need of a Savior and have acknowledged Jesus' death on the cross in their place to pay their sin debt, have been washed clean! For those who believe in Jesus as Savior, the One who rose again rising victorious over the grave once and for all, our only Way to heaven – Almighty God, you have a paradise of rest to look forward to in sure hope (Rom. 5:5)!!

Hebrews 11:10 (NLT) *Abraham was confidently looking forward to a city with eternal foundations, a city designed and built by God.*

Trusting in this sure hope with confidence brings peace.
Please read Philippians 4:6-8. _____

Instead of worry what should we do (vs. 6)?

_____

Pray! And that means as soon as we say, "Amen" we do not pick back up all our worries and be on our way! 1 Peter 5:7 tells us to cast our cares, our anxieties on Him because He cares for us! If you have ever been fishing a good cast is way out there in the water and you must let it sit way out there in the water or you won't catch anything. If we want God to handle our cares, we need to let them sit in His lap and not reel em' back into our own!

What kind of peace does God give us (vs. 7)?

_____

The kind that will go beyond our understanding and it will guard our hearts and our minds!! When we trust Him enough to let go of our illusion of control and simply receive His peace of heart and mind the world will take notice! What an opportunity to witness, to magnify our Lord to a world that so desperately craves what only He can give, a world trying to fill the void in their life that only He can fill.

According to Philippians 4:8 what should we be fixing our minds on?

_____

_____

Can you list one thing in your life to match each description listed in this verse?

true	
noble	

right	
pure	
lovely	
admirable	
excellent	
praiseworthy	

In thinking on our future home in God's eternal unshakable Kingdom please read John 14:1-4. _____

What encourages you the most in these few verses?

_____

_____

_____

As we begin to close please read Hebrews 12:18-28. _____

Please fill in the table below with the contrasting details given between the two covenants.

Hebrews 12:18-21	Hebrews 12:22-24

WOW! Praise the mighty victorious name of Jesus! *You have come to Jesus, the one who mediates the new covenant between God and people, and to the sprinkled blood, which speaks of forgiveness* (Hebrews 12:24 NLT).

Since we are receiving a Kingdom that is unshakable, let us be thankful and please God by worshiping him with holy fear and awe. Hebrews 12:28 (NLT)

Oh, dear one may you and I both grow in ever increasing amounts of trust in our Rock, our unshakable God! *In peace I will lie down and sleep, for you alone, LORD, make me dwell in safety.* Psalm 4:8 (NIV)

As we wrap up please tuck this treasure into your hearts pocket. Psalm 62:6 (NIV) *Truly he is my rock and my salvation; he is my fortress, I will not be shaken.*

Please record how God impacted your heart most today.

_____

_____

_____

_____

Day 3: Simple Faith Great Purpose

Welcome back dear friend. I know we may never have met in person or maybe we have, but you know when you pray for someone your heart just grows in fondness of them. Whether we have met or not God knows your name and that I have prayed for you and so when I call you a dear friend, I do so mean it from my heart. *Every time I think of you, I give thanks to God.* Philippians 1:3 (NLT)

Please bow in prayer as we embark today.

Jeremiah 33:3 (NI V) *'Call to me and I will answer you and tell you great and unsearchable things you do not know.'*

Do you remember Rahab? A gal we mentioned way back in week 1 day 2 of our study?! Well, as we continue in Joshua chapter 2 today, we will find ourselves crossing paths with this courageous woman of unshakable trust once more!

Please meet me on the other side of Joshua 2. _____

Here in Joshua 2:1 we see Joshua send out two spies. Ecclesiastes 4:9-12 tells us the benefit of two over one. Who has God given you as a plus one? Sometimes in certain seasons God Almighty may seem to be your only plus One. Often in those times He is equipping us to reach out and be someone else's plus one with the comfort He Himself gave us (2 Corinthians 1:4). Never underestimate even the smallest act of kindness given away. It may not matter at all but then again it might and that "might" is too valuable to side with doubt.

Joshua sends out these two SECRETLY. The last time he was part of a spy mission things did not end well back in Numbers 13-14. Maybe he was concerned about going public with the news the spies brought back should it be negative... maybe he thought the people would unkindly judge his spy plan and question his leadership ability... Whatever the reason for his approach Joshua moved forward in God's purpose. Do you have any doubts or insecurities that are preventing you from moving forward in God's plan?

_____

_____

"I am sending you out like sheep among wolves. Therefore be as shrewd as snakes and as innocent as doves. Matthew 10:16 (NIV)

In Joshua 2:3 the king of Jericho sends orders to Rahab. What are they?

_____

It seems the king assumed she would side with her community. It seems he assumed she did not really know what was going on.

Recognizing that she is depicted as a gal involved in prostitution from a pagan land how quick would you and I just assume she wouldn't be interested in hearing the Good News of Jesus?!

However as we get further into her story we see this gal, this pagan, this Canaanite whose land was cursed all the way back from the time of Noah, this prostitute named Rahab... was willing to risk EVERYTHING as she lay her unshakable trust in the God of the Israelites she had only merely heard about up until now!!

Rahab was not going to let her past get in the way of the NEW role God had for her to step into!! *Therefore, if anyone is in Christ, the new creation has come: The old has gone, the new is here!* 2 Corinthians 5:17 (NIV)

Might we pray not to let someone's appearance, lifestyle or backstory keep us from sharing the Good News of Jesus with them. *"The harvest is great, but the workers are few. So pray to the Lord who is in charge of the harvest; ask him to send more workers into his fields."* (Matthew 9:37-38 NLT)

In Joshua 2:4-5 we see a lie. We know that is never okay, truth is always the way to go as hard as it may seem at times. Considering Rahab's background, she may not have known lying to be out of the norm. However, that does not make it right.

In this particular situation I think our job is not to judge, but rather to realize God isn't expecting perfection but rather for us to make the perfect effort to do the best we can in placing our trust in His faithfulness. Rahab, I believe was giving God her perfect best and trusting with the simple faith she had that God would do GREAT things for her and her family.

Rahab speaks her confident faith in God through Joshua 2:8-12. What are some of the things Rahab trusts are true and how does she even know about these things?

_____

_____

_____

_____

Rahab is even willing to place the fate of her entire family in the hands of the Israelites God!! Interesting, that even though the Israelites, who have walked with God for decades and have experienced the power of God, it is Rahab that displays greater trust!

The enemy CLEARLY understood who was fighting for them and were beyond terrified at their fate in His mighty hands! Yet God's very own were hiding out under flax?!! Are we allowing the Truth about who our God is and who He wants to be to us to be clearer to the enemy than to our own hearts and minds?! *Listen! The LORD's arm is not too weak to save you, nor is his ear too deaf to hear you call.* Isaiah 59:1 (NLT)

I want us to pay special attention to Joshua 2:15 NLT below.

Then, since Rahab's house was built into the town wall…

Where was Rahab's house built?

_____

Into the town wall. Just tuck this gem into your pocket you will need it tomorrow.

Explain the agreement between the spies and Rahab in Joshua 2:14-21.

_____
_____
_____

_____

The spies offered their own lives as a guarantee for her safety. Rahab needed to leave the scarlet cord hanging from her window and have her entire family within her house for all to be saved when the battle hit.

God offered His Son Jesus as a sacrifice and all who put their trust in Him are guaranteed a safe arrival into His Kingdom Home!

John 12:46 (NIV) *I have come into the world as a light, so that no one who believes in me should stay in darkness.* 2 Timothy 4:18 (NLT) *Yes, and the Lord will deliver me from every evil attack and will bring me safely into his heavenly Kingdom. All glory to God forever and ever! Amen.*

I give them eternal life, and they shall never perish; no one will snatch them out of my hand. John 10:28 (NIV)

Dear one, God accomplished His divine purpose that day through the simple faith of Rahab who was willing to place unshakable trust in the Light of His redeeming Truth. May it be said of us. Please record below how God impacted your heart the most today.

_____
_____
_____

Day 4: Raise Your Ebenezer

Here we are at the end of our book but at the beginning of a new chapter in our walk with our God. A chapter I pray is much more infused with trust than the last. Faith moves in one direction, forward so let's get going!

Please begin in prayer.

When I think of all this, I fall to my knees and pray to the Father, the Creator of everything in heaven and on earth. I pray that from his glorious, unlimited resources he will empower you with inner strength though his Spirit. Then Christ will make his home in your hearts as you trust in him. Your roots will grow down into God's love and keep you strong. And may you have the power to understand, as all God's people should, how wide, how long, how high, and how deep his love is. May you experience the love of Christ, though it is too great to understand fully. Then you will be made complete with all the fullness of life and power that comes from God.

Now all glory to God, who is able, through his mighty power at work within us, to accomplish infinitely more than we might ask or think. Glory to him in the church and in Christ Jesus through all generations forever and ever! Amen. Ephesians 3:14-21 (NLT)

Yesterday we left off at the end of Joshua chapter 2. Rahab courageously stuck her neck out to protect the Israelite spies. She chose to place her trust in their God from all that she had heard about Him.
Glance back through Joshua chapter 2 and recall the item and what color it was that she was to have hanging from her window. Remember she was to do this so that her and her family's lives would to be spared.
(Hint: Joshua 2:21)

A scarlet rope.

I am reminded of the first Passover in Exodus when God spared the Israelites from the angel of death that passed over Egypt. What was to be put on the doorposts so that the angel of death would pass over them and spare the lives of their first born? Please read Exodus 12:21-23 before responding.

It was the blood of the lamb brushed on the doorposts with hyssop.

Read Isaiah 1:18 (NIV) recorded below and circle the word "scarlet".
"Come now, let us settle the matter," says the LORD. "Though your sins are like scarlet, they shall be as white as snow; though they are red as crimson, they shall be like wool.

Please read Psalm 51:7 (NIV) below and circle the word "hyssop".

Cleanse me with hyssop, and I will be clean; wash me, and I will be whiter than snow.

Rahab was to hang the scarlet cord out her window, the doorway of escape for the spies so that she would escape death! The scarlet blood of the lamb spread over the door with hyssop so the Israelites could escape death. When we confess our sin to our Lord and Savior, believing Jesus was the Lamb that was slain (Rev. 13:8) in our place and rose victorious, the Lion of Judah that has triumphed, alive today, we too escape death!!! We then stand forgiven, washed of sin, clean and white as snow!!! Oh, dear one I pray the magnitude of that never loses its wow factor in our hearts!!!

1 John 1:7 (NIV) *But if we walk in the light, as he is in the light, we have fellowship with one another, and the blood of Jesus, his Son, purifies us from all sin.*

Praise Him!!! Oh, praise Him for such redeeming grace!! *"Do not weep! See, the Lion of the tribe of Judah, the Root of David, has triumphed* (Revelation 5:5 NIV).

Let's head on over to Joshua 6 now and read that chapter. _____ It's a wild one so do not rush through it, rather savor the details as if you were there.

WOW now who needs TV when you have the Bible right!!

Joshua 6:17 tells us all will be destroyed except who?

_____

Because God keeps His promises!

Joshua 6:20 tells us what collapsed?

_____

The walls of Jericho!! Because our God is mighty!

But wait!!! Remember that verse I told you to tuck in your pocket yesterday that you would need today! It was Joshua 2:15, go back and check that verse in your notes and see just where that verse tells us Rahab's house was.

In the wall!! You mean to tell me the entire fortified wall fell EXCEPT Rahab's house which was in that same wall!!!?!

Yes! Because our God is able! Nothing is too hard for Him; His arm is not too short to save!! Mark 9:23 (NLT) *"What do you mean, 'If I can'?" Jesus asked. "Anything is possible if a person believes."*

We cannot let Joshua 6:21 go unnoticed. What weapon does it record the Israelites defeating the enemy with?

The sword! And what does the sword symbolize in the armor of God? See Ephesians 6:17.

The sword of the Spirit is the Word of God!!!!! Dear one, we win our battles with the Word of God, trusting in His sure and precious promises!!

Joshua 6:22 (NLT) is a clincher for me. *Meanwhile, Joshua said to the two spies, "Keep your promise. Go to the prostitute's house and bring her out, along with all her family."*

"Go to the house men, yes, the same house that was in the wall that came crashing down!" I imagine as the dust and smoke cleared it was quite a sight to see that one little house with the crumbled wall all around it still in pristine condition standing tall without even a scratch on it!

"Go to her men, keep your promise and BRING. HER. OUT!!!" Oh, how that gives me goosebumps all over! As promised, bring her out of all the rubble and the mess. Though the enemy would like us to believe that is where we belong when we have failed, been wronged or experienced tragedy beyond words. Micah 7:8 (NIV) clearly states, *Do not gloat over me, my enemy! Though I have fallen, I will rise. Though I sit in darkness, the LORD will be my light.*

You, dear one, are His beloved child and He has called you out by name to be set apart in this world as His chosen treasure.

(Insert your own name for "Jacob" and "Israel" in that first line below.)
But now, this is what the LORD says-he who created you, Jacob, he who formed you, Israel: "Do not fear, for I have redeemed you: I have summoned you by name; you are mine. When you pass through the waters, I will be with you; and when you pass through the rivers, they will not sweep over you. When you walk through the fire, you will not be burned; the flames will not set you ablaze. For I am the LORD your God, (Isaiah 43:1-3 NIV).

It was not only Rahab that was spared that day, the command was to bring her AND her whole family out! Her decision to place her trust in God broke the chains the enemy had not only on her, but on her entire family!!!

In 1 Samuel 7 the Israelites win a battle in the Lord's strength. Remember verse 12 (NIV) states, *Then Samuel took a stone and set it up between Mizpah and Shen. He named it Ebenezer, saying, "Thus far the LORD has helped us."*

I imagine Rahab walking out of her unshaken home, and amidst the rubble something catches her eye. It's a small rock in the shape of a heart. She stops for just a moment and stoops down to pick it up. With tears of joy escaping down her cheeks, she whispers to herself as she slips the memento into her pocket; "I am His and He is mine, I'll trust Him forever, for thus far the LORD has helped me."

When we place our trust in our God's unshakable Kingdom, we too can stand unshaken through any storm. Like Rahab, trust He will bring you through, He will bring you out. Go back to what you know to find your faith in all that you don't. Remember what you have learned in this study of Scripture about who your God is and how He loves you, how He came into this world to bring the Light of which no darkness can overcome!

John 1:5 (NIV) *The light shines in the darkness, and the darkness has not overcome it.*

Before you tuck this book back on the shelf, I encourage you to find one small rock to symbolize a steppingstone of faith, a steppingstone of remembrance. Write the word TRUST on it and place it where it will stand as a reminder to you of all that God has taught you these past 10 weeks. He is Faithful and True, a solid foundation upon which you can place your trust and stand unshaken.

Raise your "Ebenezer" for, *"Thus far the LORD has helped us."*

God bless you muchly dear one~ Janette

Day 5: At His Feet – A Time to Reflect

Today reflect over this final week of study. I encourage you to spend time with God in prayer and record on the lines below how God is tying it together and applying it to your life specifically for such a time as this.

Ask that God make it clear who He would have you invite into an opportunity to share Him, to apply what you are learning; maybe a child, grandchild, friend… trust Him to continue to take the lead. May we have a heart ever ready with eyes and ears out to the opportunities God wants to invite us into for His glory and praise.

Do not merely listen to the word, and so deceive yourselves. Do what it says. Anyone who listens to the word but does not do what it says is like someone who looks at his face in a mirror and, after looking at himself, goes away and immediately forgets what he looks like. But whoever looks intently into the perfect law that gives freedom, and continues in it – not forgetting what they have heard, but doing it – they will be blessed in what they do.
James 1:22-25 (NIV)

_____
_____
_____
_____
_____
_____
_____
_____
_____
_____

If you have not found your TRUST rock yet I encourage you to find some time today to complete that activity if you are able. This might be the perfect opportunity to invite someone along and share what you have been learning and what your TRUST rock means to you.

Philippians 4:13 (NIV) *I can do all this through him who gives me strength.*

John 14:26 (NIV) *But the Advocate, the Holy Spirit, whom the Father will send in my name, will teach you all things and will remind you of everything I have said to you.*

Day 6 & 7: At His Feet – A Time to Reflect

Over the next two days take time to review each of your completed reflection sheets on each weeks days 6 and 7. As you lay it all at His feet, praise Him for the way He has faithfully led us through. Thank Him for revealing great and unsearchable things we did not know before we began. Ask that He continue to cultivate a craving for more of Him in our hearts and minds every day. Ask that we submit to a full invasion of Him within us that we might more clearly magnify His Light to this world for His glory and praise. Record below a summary of all your most impactful points gathered from each week and ask that God imprint His trustworthiness with His very own fingerprint on your heart.

_____
_____
_____
_____
_____
_____
_____
_____
_____
_____
_____
_____
_____
_____
_____
_____

Thank you muchly~ Janette
P.S. I truly hope you will join me for the second leg of our journey through the life of Jesus in, "LIVE in The Light" book 2 in the L.I.G.H.T. series.

To him who is able to keep you from stumbling and to present you before his glorious presence without fault and with great joy – to the only God our Savior be glory, majesty, power and authority, through Jesus Christ our Lord, before all ages, now and forevermore! Amen.
Jude 1:24-25 (NIV)

ABOUT: REDEEMING GRACE 99|1 MINISTRIES

Redeeming Grace 99|1 Ministries is based on Matthew 18:12-14. There is no situation, circumstance or life God cannot reach, restore, revive and fully redeem for our good and His glory. Redeeming grace is the criminal on the cross entering into Paradise; it's Ruth the pagan becoming part of Jesus' genealogy; it's Jairus' daughter brought back to life; it's Joseph pulled from the prison and made a mighty leader; it's Daniel on the other side of the lion's den; it's Saul turned Paul; it's Jonah out of the whale; it's David and Bathsheba's son Solomon; it's Hannah having Samuel after bareness; it's the man lame for 38 years made to walk; it's five loaves and two fish becoming a meal feeding 5,000 with leftovers; it's Lazarus walking out of the tomb; it's the widow's oil that never ran out; it's the parting of the Red Sea and the reseeding of the Jordan; it's you and I realizing our need for a Savior as we look to Jesus high and lifted up, believing His death on the cross was in our place for our sin, then resurrecting from the grave God defeating the enemy of our souls once and for all. We are made new in receiving the transforming Truth of His love so that we might be made a vessel of His victory. His redeeming grace writes living hope on every page of our lives. You have never laid eyes on someone God did not love. Our mission is to reach one, and then another and another…with the Good News of His redeeming grace for us all through Jesus, raising the population of heaven by His grace, to His glory and praise.

Redeeming Grace 99|1 Ministries graphic designs © 2020
Design credit: Noah Kieffer

Author head shot photo credit: Jesse & Laura Rogers

i *NLT Parallel Study Bible* © 2011 by Tyndale House Publishers, Inc., Carol Stream, IL 60188. All rights reserved. Pg.1727-1731 (harmony of the gospels list referenced)

ii Ibid. pg. 1721

iii The *NLT Study Bible* notes copyright © 2008 by Tyndale House Publishers, Inc., Carol Stream, IL 60188. All rights reserved. Pg. 1975 (note Jn. 1:14)

iv Ibid. Pg. 1884 (note Lk. 1:3)

v Ibid. The *NLT Study Bible* notes, Pg. 1891 (note Lk. 2:26)

vi Ibid. Pg. 2054 (note Acts 7:55-58)

vii Ibid. The *NLT Study Bible* notes, Pg. 1977 (note Jn. 1:40-42)

viii Ibid. The *Life Application Study Bible* notes, Pg. 1983 (note Jn. 4:5-7)

ix Taken from the ESV® Study Bible (The Holy Bible, English Standard Version®), copyright ©2008 by Crossway, a publishing ministry of Good News Publishers. Used by permission. All rights reserved. Pg. 2029 (note John 4:46)

x Ibid. *NLT Parallel Study Bible*, Pg. 1721 (note in section "The Four Gospels")

xi Ibid. The *NLT Study Bible* notes, Pg. 1904 (note Lk. 5:36-38)

xii Ibid. The *Life Application Study Bible* notes, Pg. 1987 (note Jn. 5:27)

xiii Ibid. Pg.1768 (note Matt. 12:4)

xiv Courson, J. (2003). *Jon Courson's Application Commentary New Testament*, Thomas Nelson Inc. Nashville, Tennessee. Pg. 344 (note Lk. 8:22-25)

xv Ibid. Pg. 326 (note Lk. 6:12, 13)

xvi Ibid. Pg. 326 (note Lk. 6:14-16)